A VIEW FROM THE RIDGE

A VIEW

FROM THE

RIDGE

The Testimony of a
Twentieth-Century Christian

MORRIS WEST

HarperSanFrancisco
An Imprint of HarperCollins*Publishers*

HarperCollins Web Site: http://www.harpercollins.com

HarperCollins,® ▨,® and HarperSanFrancisco™ are trademarks of HarperCollins Publishers Inc.

FIRST EDITION

Library of Congress Cataloging-in-Publication Data

West, Morris L.
    A view from the ridge : the testimony of a twentieth-century Christian / by Morris West. — 1st ed.
        ISBN 0-06-069062-3 (cloth)
        ISBN 0-06-069381-9 (pbk.)
        1. West, Morris L.   2. Catholics—Australia—Biography.
3. Novelists, Australian—Biography.   I. Title.
BX4705.W383A3   1996
282′.092—dc20
[B]   96-28489

96 97 98 99 00 ICC\HAD 10 9 8 7 6 5 4 3 2 1

TABLE *of* CONTENTS

In Him we live and move and
have our being

ACTS XVII v.28

A VIEW FROM THE RIDGE

PROLOGUE

I have been asked, many times, to write the story of my life. I have always declined. The chronicles of my works and days have already been presented under the decent draperies of fiction.

What I offer instead is an act of witness: the testimony of a pilgrim, a fellow with a cockleshell in his hat, a staff in his hand, with eighty years of living recorded in his brainbox and his aching joints. It is also a celebration of survival and an acknowledgment of those unmerited gifts that made survival possible.

As I begin to write, I feel like a climber who, after a long and arduous ascent, has reached the high ridge of the range and now pauses to draw breath and get his courage up for the last stage of the journey.

When I look back, I see a long, gradual slope, with all its features plain: the dark forests, the green pastures, the rocky outcrops, the flashing streams, the swamps, the dangerous defiles, the post-houses, the places of ambush. The landscape is silent and empty, like a relief map set for a mock battle, but once, in truth, it was a battleground, loud with the noise of combat. I offer my salute to the fallen. I wonder what happened to other survivors. I wonder, too, why I have been spared to stand in this high place and contemplate my yesterdays.

I am surprised that the moment is so calm. Then, I remember that what I see is all gained ground. It can never be disputed again, but I can never again go back to it. I cannot even stay here in the momentary, windless calm of this high place. The pilgrimage is not over yet.

Before me, the land falls steeply into a dark valley, beyond which I see—or think I see—the lights of the city that is the goal of my pilgrimage. By any measure of time, space, or probability, I am not far away from it, but I wonder, as I have often wondered before, whether the city is not an illusion, whether its lights are not folly-fires, jack-o'-lanterns. However, I have always known that one day I should have to go down alone into the dark valley and make my own discovery of what lies on the other side.

Strange as it may seem, I am not afraid. I have accepted long since that a confession of faith is a confession of not-knowing. I have accepted to trust that the city exists, that the lights are real and that what awaits the pilgrim is a homecoming.

Prove it, I cannot. Deserve it, I do not. If my trust is proved a folly, then so be it. Life has served me as it serves everyone, sometimes well and sometimes ill, but I have learned to be grateful for the gifts of it, for the love that began it and the other loves with which I have been so richly endowed. This, let me say it plain, is no more than a simple acknowledgment of the sum of my good fortune.

I am also familiar with the tears and the terrors of human life. Sometimes it has seemed to me that the sanctions for being human are so horrendous that it is a madness to relate them to any kind of divine plan.

We are conceived without consent, wrenched whimpering into an alien universe with our death sentence already written on the palms of our helpless hands: a cancer will eat our guts, a fanatic with a sword will cut off our heads, a drunken fool will mow us down with an automobile. Sentence once passed, there may be deferment, but there is no mitigation, no commutation, no amnesty.

If I have understood nothing else in the gospel narratives, I have grasped always the tragedy of Christ's deathwatch on the Mount of Olives and his cry of utter heartbreak just before the end: "My God, my God, why have you abandoned me?"

This is what pushes us toward despair: the sheer indifference of the universe, the lunatic aspect of a cosmos with no known beginning, no intelligible end, and no apparent meaning to its brutal dynamics. I believe that it is this despair which breeds the cruelties we practice upon one another. Evil is a destructive monotony in our lives. We can become so hardened to its obscenity that it does not move us anymore. On the other hand, the older I get, the more I am confirmed in the conviction that all the saving graces in our lives are delivered to us in random moments of simple revelation: the smile of a sleeping child, the lined face of an old grandmother dozing in the sun.

The fact is, we can survive only in communion, with our present, with our past, and with our dusty, footsore fellows on the road. We are all haunted by a poetry of living: by lullabies half-remembered, the sound of train whistles in the night, the scent of lavender in a summer garden. We are haunted, too, by grief and terror and memories of random cruelty and the macabre dissolutions of age.

Yet I am sure that it is in this domain of our daily experience that the Creator establishes communion with us. This is where the radical mystery of the Incarnation reenacts itself: the living God made flesh and dwelling among us, engaging us in our own tongue and in the symbols of our daily lives.

This, I most firmly believe, is how revelation is most commonly given to us. Human experience always outstrips our capacity to communicate it. Our commonest symbols convey different meanings in different cultures. Our creeds are expressed in words that belong to other ages, other stages of knowledge, other climates of experience. Do you remember how, in the book of Judges, the men of Galaad asked the man of Ephraim to identify himself? They asked him to say a single word, "Shibboleth." He pronounced it "Sibboleth." So they seized him and killed him at the Jordan ford.

I write, therefore, at a constant risk of misinterpretation or misunderstanding. I accept the risks; I beg your patience and tolerance. I do not seek to impose my opinions on you. God forbid! I seek only to share my thoughts before I step down into the silence of the dark valley.

I have no new truths to tell you. I live as you do, enveloped in ancient mysteries. I stand in church on Sunday and recite the ancient creedal formula: "I believe in one God the Father Almighty, creator of heaven and earth, and in Jesus Christ, His only Son, our Lord. I believe in the Holy Spirit, the Lord, the giver of life, who proceeds from the Father and the Son . . ." I have no idea how this triune deity presents itself to, or is apprehended by, the woman standing next to me.

We make together the affirmation that is more ancient than the creed itself. "Christ died. Christ is risen. Christ will come again." The dying is history. The resurrection is hearsay from witnesses long dead. The coming is a promise long deferred. We affirm them as the basic premises of our faith, yet we cannot explain them, certainly we cannot prove them by any rules of evidence, and more than half the human race dismisses them as superstition.

The old divines talked about the gift of faith. It seems to me that there is an earlier gift, a desire, an openness to receive the light when and if it is offered. This openness is a quality of perception like poetry or divination or the wonderful imagination of a happy child.

If you have not the grace—or if you have lost it or mislaid it—you are thrust back on reason, noblest of the faculties, said the old Greeks, but no key to the mystery and the paradox and the tragedy of the human condition. On the contrary, reason may become an executioner's ax or an atomic trigger unless the reasons of the heart are spoken to protest the tragic nonsense of human syllogisms. These are the thoughts, the occasional insights, I want to share with you before I take my leave and go down into the silence of the dark valley. Let me begin with my own affirmation as a Christian in this millennial decade.

What has been left to us? The imprint of the Maker's hand on every stone and shard and living tissue on the planet; the simplicity of Jesus' repeated message, "A new commandment I give to you, that you love one another"; and finally the promise of the abiding Spirit, the enlightener, the comforter, which, like the wind, breathes where it will, ruffling alike the wheat fields of the homestead and what, in our tribal arrogance, we sometimes call the alien corn.

What you must not expect from me in this book is a formal narrative, a connected argument about what I believe and do not believe. I have neither taste nor time for polemics. The details of a life as long as mine become elusive. The dimension of time becomes fluid. Past, present, and future meld into one another like the currents of the water that I watch every day from my study window. Every time I attempt to record them with pen or paintbrush, they have changed before I make the first stroke.

There is no confusion in this. There is only a sense of unity, continuity, magical variety—and this is one of the rewards of age that I would like to share with you.

I have had a strange life, but a rich and rewarding one. By nature, I am an optimistic man. By nurture, I am disposed to religious belief. That earns me no special merit, but I have paid a high price for whatever gifts came with it.

I was born into an Irish-Australian Catholic family at a time when the Irish memory of persecution was still vivid, when advertisements for staff in my hometown still carried the phrase "No Catholics, no Irish, no Jews need apply." I was taught by scholars who valued learning because their forefathers had been taught in the hedge schools of Ireland. Our pastors were men who had left their homeland to keep faith alive in a far and alien country founded as a penal colony. We were an excluded and exclusive community. We learned at least basic charity because we had mutual need of it. We learned rough politics because we had to claw our way to influence in a community still dominated by the Imperial English.

When I was very young, not yet fourteen, I joined, as a postulant, the Congregation of the Brothers of the Christian Schools of Ireland, my old teachers. My family life was not happy; my father and mother were separated. Still, I could not complain of a lack of love, because I had it in full measure in the extended Irish family. On my part, the decision was an act of fugue. On the part of the Congregation, it was part of a program called "fostering vocations" but, in fact, as I see it now, a seduction of the young and immature into a choice that they were quite unready to make.

My sojourn in the Congregation lasted twelve years and ended on the eve of my final vows with an agonized decision to return to a world of which I was almost totally ignorant. In the religious life, I met a few saints, a number of emotional cripples, some brilliant scholars, a largish number of men as ordinary as myself, and a small number of malicious folk, whom, even today, I cannot remember without a pang of resentment. Myself, I was not made for a monk. I was restless, unsatisfied, irked by obedience and celibacy; but I served honorably under the terms of the vows I had made. The record of my abdication is clear: I declined to continue.

The theology that was preached to us was the old Triden-tine codex: Scripture and Tradition. The sole authentic reposi-tory of tradition, the sole arbiter of faith and morals, was the Church—Holy, Roman, Catholic, and Apostolic. Modernists were damned along with Lutherans, Anabaptists, and ancient Donatists. When Catholics were persecuted, they were mar-tyrs. When Simon de Montfort slaughtered the Albigensians, he was a godly knight extirpating a foul heresy. Deeply condi-tioned though I was, I could not swallow so hairy a camel, so to my emotional unrest was added a ferment of intellectual doubts.

What is relevant to this reckoning is that, in the Congregation, I had my first experience of techniques designed to wash the human brain and bend the human spirit. They were practiced by my novice master, who, though he is long dead, I still regard as an ignorant and coarse man, psychologically maimed, anti-intellectual, spiritually blind, who did grave and sometimes irreparable damage to many of the youths in his charge.

He humiliated them with gross penances: shaving their heads, sentencing them to extra field labor, making them take meal after meal on their knees. He bullied them at lecture time. He tyrannized them with spiritual fears: damnation in every sexual thought, double damnation for every impulse of pride or revolt. I loathed him then. I pity him now, but when-ever I soften too much, I remember some pale and pitiful youth, twitching and gibbering in a subacute psychosis that our mentor dismissed as "just another case of scruples." He was the first official intimidator I met. I have hated the breed ever since, be they Marxists, Fascists, bureaucrats, or bullying army sergeants.

And yet, I learned much from him. I learned to be silent and to wait. I learned the futility of argument with the deaf. I learned never to confuse the truth with the man who preached or perverted it, to suspect always the wild evangelist who cries, "Heaven is this way. Follow me and I will get you there." My trade is words, and I discovered early how many contradictions can be read into a single simple text.

There was one more harsh lesson. My novice master was a loveless man. He had never experienced love; therefore, he could not give it. So he lived out his life by text and rote and ritual. With males, he was always in contest; with women, although he was a big, athletic fellow, he was so afraid that he scuttled away when they approached. I prayed I would never be like him. I knew that I could never believe in the God he preached. To reach the calm in which, thank God, I now reside, I have had to learn to forgive him.

What I cannot forgive, and what I can never condone, is the impersonal cruelty that institutions—my own church among them—practice upon their members and that they justify by a thousand arguments, none of which I find acceptable. I have fought this cruelty all my life. I hold firmly to the gospel message that authority is given for service and not for the exercise of power. Magistracy is a function of ministry; all other use of it is a perversion.

Do I believe in God? Yes, I do, though I cannot reason Him into existence, though I do not believe all that is written, or approve all that is done, in His name. I believe that all creation is a mask of God and that the most diverse creeds cloak an essential truth.

What do I believe about man? That he is a malicious animal and sometimes a mad one. That he is improvable but never, never perfectible. That brutality will debase him, and only love and respect and forgiveness can ennoble him.

I do not believe in the disciplines of fear. I am constantly shocked by the many who find them acceptable. They haunt me like the ghosts of Belsen jailers. Human existence is harsh and dangerous, and there are no easy answers to its dilemmas. God is not everywhere, or always, in evidence in his own creation. It is this seeming absence that is the hardest test of faith and hope and love.

No creed defines God. No creed can define God. No set of laws, no system of moralities, can contain or control the mass of human animals upon the planet driven by the primal instinct of survival. The mystery is that human beings seek God as a seed planted in the dark earth thrusts its shoot upward to expose itself to the sun. It is this instinctive seeking of the life force, this turning toward the source of being, that is the nature of human experience. It is what makes birth important and dying an appropriate coda to life.

Our Lord did not invent the codex of canon law. He did not dictate the *Summa* of Thomas Aquinas. He sat upon a hillside, perched himself in a rocking boat just off the beach. He spoke in the synagogues and in the houses of the people. The images he used were the simplest images of rural life: flowers and sheep and grain and weeds growing among wheat. He taught his followers to acknowledge the unknown God as "Father." I have felt very often that we Christians have divided ourselves because we have tried to elaborate too much upon the majestic simplicity of the message given to us. We have denied ourselves by legislation the liberty of the children of God. We have alienated ourselves one from another like the builders of the Tower of Babel because we have not known the things that conduce to our peace.

We have to admit, first to ourselves, and then, very humbly, to one another, that we live at the heart of a dark mystery, which we can still only describe by allegory and legend or the sterile and incomplete formulae of physical science.

The act of faith is not a leap from darkness into light. It is an affirmation that light exists beyond darkness, that the chaos and the cruelties of existence do, in the end, make sense, and that the primal act of creation, with all that issued from it, was an act of love.

The strongest compulsion to belief is not reason but need. We cannot endure to live in a mad universe. We are compelled, for our own sanity, to make sense of it. Sooner or later we are forced either to blasphemy or to the pilgrim search for the source of light—the shrine where creative love resides.

This opening of the Self to the Other, the Creature to the Creator, is the first step along the winding road, the first qualification for the promised gift: "Seek and you shall find, knock and the door shall be opened to you . . ."

CHAPTER 1

THE TEMPLES
of the STRANGERS

One of the earliest questions that presented itself to my youthful mind was that of election: Why had God chosen the Jewish people as the sole recipients of His divine revelation and of the messianic promise? By what creative caprice had he excluded all others? Later, the question became more particular. Why was I among those chosen, not merely to receive a new revelation of Christian faith, but to spread it as an evangelist, thus filling up the gaps in a whimsical design. I was not yet cynical enough to ask by what right my parents had pledged my allegiance to a god or an institution while I was a week-old infant. So, at first I accepted on faith the answer I was given: that the Almighty in his infinite wisdom had so disposed it.

My earliest education thus grounded me in prejudice, which means prejudgment, unexamined conviction. My later training as a novice was—let me say it baldly—an exercise in bigotry. All non-Christians were either pagans or infidels. Christians who were not in communion with Rome were conveniently, if inaccurately, classified as heretics or schismatics. Mixed marriages were not only frowned upon but actively discouraged and diminished by truncated ceremonies. The faith history we were taught was heavily expurgated, and inquiry into historic forgeries and scandals was discouraged. We were still living in the stormy afterglow of Pope Pius X, who had exacted of all clergy the oath against "modernism," who had harassed scholars and intellectuals to such a degree that his successor, Benedict XV, had to call an official halt to the battle between hard-line traditionalists and the so-called modernists.

Pius X had died in 1914, and Benedict XV reigned until 1922, but climates in the church change very slowly, and even in the late twenties and thirties candidates from the priesthood were obliged, before ordination, to take a formal oath abjuring modernist errors.

Our Irish superiors discouraged us from any interest in these matters. We were not clerics. We had no authority in the Church. We were laymen under vows—dominies, charged to pass on ancient certainties, not to raise doubts or debates among our young charges. We were not philosophers or theologians or historians. These high matters were best left to the Dominicans, the Jesuits, the Benedictines. I tell you all this not to raise the clamor of old battles—or modern ones—but only to point out that every age and every religion has its extremists and its literalists. Their influence is divisive and destructive. The conditioning of their disciples is generally very thorough. The deprogramming is not always successful.

My teaching career began in 1934 in a large community of twenty-odd brethren who served three schools in the suburbs of Sydney. That was, one way and another, a year of world-shaking events: Hitler, then chancellor of Germany, staged the "Night of the Long Knives," a killing spree that wiped out all effective opposition to his regime. Dollfuss was assassinated in Austria; Mao Tse-tung began the Long March in China.

In our small, suburban enclosure, the echoes of these events were muted to the murmur of distant thunder. We had no radio. We juniors were forbidden to read secular newspapers.

The Catholic press of the day was notoriously parochial and partisan. The effect of this censorship on me was a slow ferment of doubt and discontent.

I was no longer the unquestioning subject, the wholehearted believer in every jot and tittle of the law. Yet, the more doubts I had, the more I felt obliged to resolve them for myself. My problems were my own. I could not, should not, load them on others. I must render the bond-service I had vowed. What I did not understand was that I had been robbed of my own fragile identity and I dared not yet reject the religious artifact that had been given to me instead.

Even so, it was not until the end of 1939, when I was due to pronounce my final and irrevocable vows, that I decided I could not continue. The school year was over. Outside, a world war had begun. I had no idea what that world held for me. All I knew was that I had to leave the Congregation and somehow, somewhere, begin a new life. It should have been a moment of liberation; however, even after I had walked out of the gates of the college, the liberation was not complete. I truly did not know who I was, or where I was going. My family were strangers to me. I had not seen them for nearly a decade. They lived six hundred miles away. I could not command enough courage that day to make the train journey. There was war in Europe, but its echoes were still muted, and I had been taught that I was engaged in a more primal struggle, against the world, the flesh, and the devil. I was a captive still, but now I was in solitary confinement. In a very real sense, I lacked even a language to communicate myself in this new and alien chaos.

I spent that night in the house of friends. I do not remember what was said or how I conducted myself. All I know is that, when I went to bed and switched off the light, I found myself sobbing uncontrollably. I was still weeping when the door of the bedroom opened and one of the daughters of the house, a young woman of my own age, came into the room.

In the morning she was gone. Two days later I was gone, too, rattling in an overcrowded train back to the home-place I had left twelve years before. I was still lost and fearful, but I knew that a small fragment of the mosaic of my lost identity had been restored. It was, and still is, like the first gleam of starfire through the black murk of storm clouds. I have always been grateful to the woman who gave it to me.

Between me and the peace in which I now dwell were many more painful journeys: the years of war, a failed marriage, an obsessively successful business life in radio, a breakdown, a risky career change, a second marriage (a successful one this time), twenty years of life away from my homeland, a long battle to maintain my bill of complaints against injustice in the Church and my right to raise my voice within it. Like Teilhard de Chardin, I had to confess that, though I loved the Church in which I was born and baptized, I could not live with her in peace. It took me a long time to understand that a community of believers is never peaceful. It is always quarrelsome and abrasive. Even the disciples of our Lord quarreled among themselves. The peace of the comforting Spirit comes strangely and quietly, like the first wonders of childhood: hold a shell to your ear and you will hear the murmurs of all the oceans of the world.

For me, the first real liberation was travel. I remember the first exotic reek of Asia, as I stood on the deck of an old Greek tub that was nosing its way into the Singapore roads at midnight. I remember the rattle of the anchor chains as we dropped the hook among the shattered corals and the rusting hulks in the harbor of Massawa, the Red Sea port from which the Italians had invaded Abyssinia. But my impressions were always skewed a little—Abyssinia was not the Kingdom of Haile

Selassie, it was the Empire of Prester John. Singapore was not the swampy outpost of Empire that Raffles had founded but the gateway to the Spice Islands, the route of the first Spanish and Portuguese and Dutch navigators who opened the seaways to far Cathay. Geography, history, and the cults of man were for me one continuous tapestry.

I recall most vividly one long Aegean summer during which my family and I cruised in our own vessel, the *Salamandra d'Oro,* a whole chaplet of islands: the green coast of Euboea, Skiathos, Skopelos, Skiros, then down through a wild storm to the Kikladhes. When the meltemi started to blow—and God, how it blew that summer!—we sheltered in the small harbor of Tinos and joined the throng of pilgrims to the Church of the Annunciation, where there is a miraculous icon of the Virgin of Good Tidings.

We were unprepared, for either the crowds or the almost suffocating atmosphere of religious expectation. Tinos is the Lourdes of the Byzantine Church. Cures are wrought there, and that year they told us that a girl, blind from birth, had miraculously recovered her sight. We did not see the girl, but the fervor and faith of the believers was in hourly evidence as they climbed the cobbled steps toward the shrine. Some of them made the ascent on their knees. Once again, I was conscious that the numen of ancient beliefs still clings to modern sanctuaries.

Mykonos was history in reverse. Once it had been an Island of the Dead; because on the island of Delos, sacred to Apollo and Artemis, no births were permitted and no deaths either. Now, there was more life here than on any of the Aegean Islands: tourists from the cruise ships, hippies from half the world sleeping on the beaches, camped on the hillside round the windmills and the white votive chapels, built mostly by sailors who had survived the perils of the sea. The harbor was an ill-tempered place, with little shelter from the wind or the swell, and skippers, cursing at one another as they battled to tie up for the night, scraped paint from their hulls and bruised their bulwarks along the crowded quay. We were glad to be gone and to run down to Delos, nosing our way carefully into the old sacred port, where there is a sign carved into the ancient pavement. It points the way to the Temples of the Strangers. The Delian games, which were celebrated every four years in the month of May, were held in honor of the God Apollo and his twin sister, Artemis, the beautiful huntress. But the Egyptians were there, too, with their own gods, Anubis and Serapis, who lived side by side with the deities of Syria. The ancient Greeks were wise enough to keep all their gods separate and their quarrels confined to the wineshops and the brothels along the waterfront.

The meltemi drove us south again through the narrow pass between Paros and Naxos. We spent an uneasy night rolling in a heavy swell under the lee of Ios and then sailed into the awesome black crater of Santorini. For the sailor, this is a strange and fearful place. In the center of the crater is a tumble of black, barren lava. The water around it is still hot and sulfurous, and the barnacles die on the hull of the vessel. There is no anchorage here except on a small submerged shelf discovered by the British Navy. The rest of the crater is thousands of feet deep, the water dark and menacing, covered with floating pumice. One can easily believe that lost Atlantis lies drowned in the dark crater. For yachtsmen, there is uneasy docking at the end of a small jetty, above which the cliffs of ash and pumice rise sheer to the mountaintop and the town. The only way up is on foot—if you want a heart attack!—or by donkey, which is guaranteed to give you a sore tail, fleas, and bruised shins from the rough buttress walls of the rampway. At night, if you sleep on board, you lurch and grind against the fenders of your neighbors, and the deck watch gets quietly drunk on ouzo or the sweet local wine.

From Santorini, with the wind abeam, we made the long reach to Rhodes, where the harbor was safe but noisy and the officials surly and the tourist food varied from eatable to abominable. For all the riches of its history, the beauty of the hinterland, the interest of the old crusader town, I was glad to be gone and to beat up past Simi to the Turkish coast—almost deserted, even in the height of summer—where every bay seemed to have its own private ruin, inhabited only by a shepherd family, where you could dive among the blocks and potsherds left by the ancient builders.

But even here, there are traps for the unwary sailor. The wind drops briefly at sundown, then, just as you think you are snug for the night, it whistles down the defiles, funneling into a full gale, and you are up all night, because the anchor drags in the sandy ground and you have to cast and cast again until you find a patch of mud and weed that will hold the hook and keep you off the rocks. Three nights of this, and you are red-eyed, irritable, and eager to make harbor, where you can rest and fill the water tanks and buy fresh food in the marketplace. It was in this mood of restrained desperation that we came to the place that, of all the islands, has remained, for me, the most vivid and most soothing memory: the Island of Kos.

It is a small place, but even in ancient times it was famous as a resort and a place of healing. The poet Horace recommended Koan wine and shrimps as the best cure for a hangover. Koan silk was so fine and transparent that it was worn by emperors and very expensive courtesans, and the bawdy proverb was that no Koan woman could swear that she was not naked even when she was dressed. However, it seems that the silkworms of Kos were fed, not on mulberry leaves, but on ash and oak and terebinth, and that, in spite of its reputation, the silk was coarser than that produced in China. Theocritus, the poet, wrote in Kos about his love for the goatherd Lycidas. Centuries later the French traveler Porqueville proclaimed, "There is no pleasanter land under heaven than Kos; and, looking at its beautiful perfumed gardens, you would say that it is an earthly paradise."

But Kos had greater claims to fame than natural beauty. It was sacred to Asclepius, the god of medicine and healing. His temple, which was also a hospital and university, was built among the pinewoods—three great tiers of it—open to the cooling winds of the sea. People came in pilgrimage from all over the Mediterranean to make their offering to the god, to drink from the sacred spring, to submit themselves to treatment by the doctor-priests.

Here, in the fourth century B.C., was born the man who is called the Father of Medicine: Hippocrates. Here, he served as a physician and a teacher and wrote at least part of the eight great treatises ascribed to him. Here was proclaimed one of the great documents of Greek civilization, the Hippocratic Oath, which expresses the fundamental ethic of the healer:

> To my master in the healing art I shall pay the same respect as to my parents and I shall share my life with him and pay all my debts to him. . . . I will use my power to help the sick to the best of my talent and judgment. . . . I will not give a fatal drink to anyone, even if it is demanded of me, nor will I suggest the giving of such drink. I will give no women the means of procuring an abortion. I will be chaste and holy in my life and actions. . . . Whenever I enter a house I shall help the sick and never shall I do harm or injury. . . . Whatever I see or hear, either in my profession or in private, I shall never reveal. All secrets shall be safe with me. . . .

Standing among the ruins of the shrine, where once the patients slept on goatskins and waited for the visitation of the sacred serpents, I was seized with a sensation of awe that has never wholly deserted me. The air was full of the scent of pine and wild thyme and basil and rosemary and flowering mint, herbs from which the priest-healers distilled their potions and whose perfume lulled the devotees, still half-drunk from the "experience of the god."

In the temple hospital of Kos, they were as concerned with the diseases of the mind as with the diseases of the body. The treatments that were prescribed bear a striking resemblance to those still in use in modern mental therapy. The patients, were they rich enough, were received into an atmosphere of religious calm and solemnity. They were lodged in an ambiance of natural beauty, between the forest and the sea. They drank at the sacred spring. They offered a sacrifice to petition the god for healing. They were soothed with opiates. Their confidence was restored by the knowledge that they were under divine tutelage and that while they slept, the god himself might visit them in the form of a sacred serpent. There is evidence also of a form of shock treatment in which, after appropriate preparation, the patient was taken blindfolded into a sacred place and perhaps heard the thunderous voice of the divinity itself.

After this experience, they went into convalescence in a dormitory or a private cell, where they rested, ate and drank lightly, and were entertained by hired musicians. Then, the rhythms of their psychic lives restored, they went away and told of all the wonders they had seen.

So great was the veneration for Kos and its Asclepion that the Emperor Claudius issued an edict absolving it from all imperial taxes. His own physician, Xenophon, was born on the island. However, it would appear that the physicians of Kos were no less corruptible than some of their modern counterparts. Xenophon, the physician, gave his imperial master poison and, when he vomited it up, tickled his throat with an envenomed feather, so that the emperor died very painfully indeed.

There are some other oddities about Kos as well, as indeed there are about most sacred places. The great sculptor Praxiteles, wishing to do honor to the island, made a copy of his image of Aphrodite, which he had modeled on the body of his mistress. The Koans were shocked by its nudity. They sent it back with an indignant note saying that they would accept it only when it was properly dressed. A modern wit has suggested that they were more interested in shepherd boys and Olympic athletes!

I have to record other oddities as well. I never could buy a Kos lettuce, and Koan wine, far from curing hangovers, is most mightily conducive thereto. The girls don't wear Koan silk anymore, and the local tourist guides who sell you little bundles of healing plants have only the haziest idea of their properties. I have pressed in my diary herbs for asthma, diarrhea, making glue, stopping hemorrhages, curing indigestion, increasing virility, and making caper sauce. Of course, one shouldn't expect them to work. They need an accompanying magic, a formula of faith, hope, and mystery long since lost to us. But the haunting still happens. Sometimes in a daydream, I find myself standing in the "sea green dawn" on the topmost terrace of the temple and listening to a ghostly voice that proclaims, "I swear by Apollo the Healer, by Asclepius, by Health and all the powers of healing, and I call to witness all the gods and goddesses that I may keep this Oath and Promise to the best of my ability and judgment. . . ."

That daydream of an ancient Mediterranean world evokes others. I remember the small gilded spirit house outside my first lodging place in Thailand, where every day I laid a fresh flower to honor the guardians and protectors of the place. I did not know who they were, but as my hosts described them, they seemed very much like the guardian angels who, my mother told me, watched over my sleep in childhood.

I remember my campfire contacts, during the Pacific War, with our own Aboriginal people, whose existence on this southern continent goes back at least fifty thousand years. They have no written language, but their cosmology is both complex and beautiful. It claims no possession of the earth but rather a possession by the earth out of which they sprang and that nourished them for millennia. They have no temples, only sacred places where the treasures of their Dreamtime memory are preserved in a special fashion.

I remember the tranquillity of the monastery garden at Tenryu-ji where I first began to understand the concordances between Christianity and Buddhism. Later, I tried to expand and celebrate them in my novel *The Ambassador*, which is, in part, the story of the assassination of President Diem of Vietnam and, in part, the story of the ambassador who connived at it. In his later despair, he turns to his old Zen master:

"Can you tell me what has happened to me?"

"I think I can. You are like the old-time traveler who sets out to make the journey from Kyoto to Edo, which, everyone tells him, is full of interest and diversity. He begins very confidently; he has money in his purse, good clothes, stout limbs and companions to lighten the journey. But before the journey is over he finds he has miscalculated. The inns are expensive, the girls are grasping, he is cheated by ferrymen and clever rogues. So, long before he reaches Edo, he has no money, his clothes are too light for the coming winter, his companions have dropped off along the way, and he is in a province whose dialect he does not understand. He is older too. Time is shorter. When he talks to the girls in the tea-houses, his heart is still at home. When he watches the merchants haggle, he knows that gold is soon spent and silk wears out. What does he do? He wants to kill himself, but he lacks the courage. He wishes he were a clever rogue like those he has met on his journey. But for this he has neither taste nor talent. He sits down by the roadside and weeps for himself. But after a while there are no more tears to shed. He hears the gongs from the monastery and he sees the maples-in-flame and he says: 'Here is light and the compassion of the Compassionate One.' But he finds no light because light is a gift to each separate man. It is not held in common. And the compassion cannot touch him, because he clings to his own guilt and will not be forgiven. Does my parable tell the true story, Amberley-san?"

"It is true. But is it ended there—the traveler motionless, without tears, lacking light, refusing compassion? There is a word for that in the West; *accidie:* it signifies the false and terrible Nirvana which is founded not on union but on separation, not on the extinction of desire but on contempt for it. And this is where I find myself now. This I think is why I cannot continue the *mondo* with you."

"There is another end to the parable, my friend. If you will be patient a little longer, I will try to show it to you. We are left, are we not, with our traveler, all alone by the roadside, bereft. He cannot go back; there is nothing to urge him forward. But, without desire, he continues walking. By the side of the road he sees an image of the Buddha, of the Goddess Kwannon, of Rai-jin the Thunder-God, a *fumiejesu,* perhaps, or even the Great Bear of the Ainu people. It is a dead thing of wood or stone or baked clay which, for our traveler, has no meaning. But, because he is a man, he knows the image has a meaning for other men: an expression of their need and their desire for enlightenment, harmony and elevation above the self. He stops by the image which has no meaning for him. He recites a prayer in whose efficacy he does not believe: 'If there be light, show me light. If there be power extend it to me. If there be forgiveness, forgive. If there be tomorrow grant me a hope in it; and if there be these things, but not for me, give me the patience to endure the not having.'"

"And how will I know if the prayer is answered?"

"When you have the courage to live without an answer."

"But if I have no courage?"

"Then you will walk just a little further along the road and you will come to a habitation of men."

"How can I be sure of that?"

"Because where there are images, there are always men!"

"And then?"

"Then you will see what the Lord Buddha saw: an old man, a sick man, a dead man, and a man with a shaven head who has no home. And then you will say; none of these is more fortunate than I; so why should I complain? And then you will either accept to live again in the habitation of men, or you will join the homeless one and continue on the road. And so, either way, your prayer will be answered and there will be a beginning of light and a desire for more light."

"And forgiveness? Who forgives me for what I have done?"

"The dead man whom you bury, the sick man whom you succor, the old man whom you support, the homeless one whose loneliness you share."

"And the image?"

"Is still an image of the Unknown and the Unknowable who may, one day, choose to enlighten you—for the All-Enlightened One has pity on mankind."

CHAPTER 2

TURNING POINTS

Turning one's life about is rather like turning a small ship in a bad sea. Do it too fast and you will broach. The wind and the waves will lay you over on your beam-ends, and you will sink. I have had some bad moments at sea, but none so threatening as those dark nights of the soul in which there is neither moonlight nor starlight but only a silent blackness. However, the crises of yesteryear are hard to share. The time frames have shifted. The geography has changed. These shifts and changes reflect themselves in this present narrative. I find myself in a wandering stream of consciousness. I am obliged to go with the current, recalling the past, examining the present, dreaming the future. I cannot, in this instance, submit myself to the disciplines of time and logic. As things come to me, I set them down, trusting that the underlying continuity—the continuity of my essential self—will emerge for the reader.

I've given up asking people, "Do you remember?" I've had too many shocks, as fellows with gray hair and potbellies, or matrons with marriageable daughters, remind me, "For God's sake! I wasn't even born then!"

I remember the year 1934 because I was then eighteen years old. I was on my first mission as a professed religious in the Congregation of the Brothers of the Christian Schools of

Ireland, in one of the inner suburbs of Sydney. I was full of zeal and innocence, woefully ignorant of what was going on in the world—which, one way and another, was quite a lot.

The Japanese installed Pu Yi puppet emperor of Manchukuo. Russia and Finland signed a ten-year nonaggression pact. Hitler and Mussolini met in Venice. Chancellor Dollfuss was murdered in Austria. King Alexander of Yugoslavia was assassinated in Marseilles, and Hitler was confirmed by plebiscite as Führer of Germany. Marie Curie died, and, unbeknownst to any of us, Sophia Loren was born.

I was teaching basic skills in reading, writing, mathematics, geography, and social deportment and the rudiments of Christian belief to forty-odd third graders, most of them from urban industrial areas with a mixed population of Anglo-Saxon, Irish, Greek, and Italian immigrant stock. Our community served three schools and numbered, if my memory serves me right, some twenty-odd brothers, among them the subject of this cautionary tale, Brother Avellino.

He was a tubby fellow, with a bald pate and black eyes and an ever-ready smile. I still had the bloom of the novitiate on me and the veil of innocence draped over my head, so I missed the shrewdness in the eyes and the facile shift of the smile and the extraordinary mobility of his opinions—yea one moment, nay the next, a saving "maybe" if the mood of the audience seemed uncertain. I also missed the cautionary comment of the Senior Member: "Avellino? I've served three terms with him now, in three different communities. Never tell him a secret that you don't want told all over town. He's everyone's man but always his own—and he's as shrewd as a Kerry horse-coper."

Avellino taught the form above mine, so we worked in adjoining classrooms. Each of us had a choir in training for the City of Sydney Eisteddfod, in which choirs and soloists from all over the state competed every year. We were considerate of each other. Each kept his classroom very quiet while the other was rehearsing his singers. We were also discreetly critical, noting examples of ragged phrasing, poor attack, bad intonation. I was too much the junior, too recently trained in monastic manners, to announce my opinions, but, as the weeks passed, I began to nurture a fair hope that I might not only beat Avellino at choir work but even have a chance of winning our section of the eisteddfod.

There were no tape recorders in those days. We didn't even have a piano in the classroom. For four days a week we sang unaccompanied, using a pitch pipe and a tuning fork to set the key. On the fifth day we had an hour in the music room with an accompanist. In between, I would run the pieces over and over in my head—an obsessional exercise in musical memory.

The obsession, however, ran more deeply and darkly than I dreamed. The eisteddfod was a public competition, an open test of my untested abilities. I wanted desperately to qualify for the finals. Even if I didn't win, I wanted to be there, to step for a brief moment out of the anonymity of conventual life and have other people confirm to me who I was, or who I dreamed I might be.

Under the system then prevailing, I had been recruited as a postulant at age thirteen and had spent four years in tutelage before taking my first annual vows. Such identity as I had was uncertain and fragile. All my social reflexes were as conditioned as those of Pavlov's dogs. My convictions had been handed to me ready-made. I had no critical apparatus at all.

Came the day when I was absolutely convinced that I had a real chance at the prize. The headmaster, who was also the Brother Superior of the community, paid me one of his rare compliments. With an unexpected grace, Brother Avellino conceded defeat. His own group was no match for mine. He was withdrawing it from the competition.

From that moment I coveted the prize with an urgency I would not have believed possible. My passion infected the choir itself and the whole class. We were an elite of the elite, almost as important as the school football team. We invented games for ourselves—a burst of four-part harmony in the middle of an arithmetic lesson, a round to finish an afternoon English period. It was all good clean fun, and we knew, with the serenity of total faith, that the prize was just at our fingertips.

Then I fell sick, very sick. The doctor was called. He diagnosed double pneumonia. My monastic cell was at that time a glassed-in verandah, cold and drafty. Hurriedly, one of the other juniors was moved into it, and I was lodged inside, to be cared for by the housekeeper, who, whatever her nursing abilities, was certainly a cure for concupiscence! Those were the days before antibiotics, so my recovery was slow. Brother Avellino took over my classes, managing some eighty boys like a roly-poly sentinel at the communicating door.

He took over my choir, too, and in the evening bouts of fever I remember his voice, soothing as a sea breeze, delivering his reports: "There's nothing to worry about. They're in splendid voice, singing like angels. All you have to do is get better, and we'll walk away with the prize!"

I was sick. I was young and stupid. I was innocent still. I missed the plural pronoun *we*. On the other hand, why should I have adverted to it anyway? A choir was a collective. A religious community was a collective. *I*, so my masters had taught me, was a dangerous literal; all their training was designed to suppress it, debase it to petty currency.

So, full of faith and confidence, I moved from illness to convalescence. I saw no sinister possibilities in the fact that I was forbidden to return to the classroom for at least two weeks after my release from confinement. I knew I was weak and unsteady.

I was happy in the fraternal support of the community and the friendship of Brother Avellino in particular.

On the other hand, I wasn't too happy with the sounds I heard during choir practice. I knew Brother Avellino had a tin ear, but I was confident that with the eisteddfod still a month away I could whip the group back into shape in a week. They had to present only two pieces. We had ample time to repolish the performance.

So I caught up on my reading, strolled in the garden, rested in the afternoons, and joined the brothers for evening chapel. When the two weeks were up, the doctor pronounced me fit for duty. I moved back to my old drafty verandah. The Brother Superior handed me a new teaching roster. It showed that I would take Brother Avellino's class for one period a day, while he took mine for choir practice. He had, it seemed, taken over the choir and would present it at the eisteddfod. I was devastated. I demanded to know why. The Brother Superior reminded me coldly that I was a man under obedience and he was not obliged to offer me any explanation for his actions. I protested that he owed me both courtesy and charity. His answer was curt. I was still a junior in religious life. I should remember the lessons of my novice master and bow my neck under the yoke of discipline. I should never, never cling to anything so tightly that I would be unhappy to let it go. I should never covet anything so much that I would commit sin to get it. And I was in sin, was I not, however venially, for questioning the judgment of my lawful superior, for wanting the worldly satisfaction of a stage appearance, for lack of charity to Brother Avellino, who had shouldered the burden of my classes for nearly six weeks and had earned the right to this small concession on my part. I should go to the chapel, beg forgiveness for my faults, and pray for light to understand the wisdom of what had been done.

My visit to the chapel produced a small light: a boyhood memory of my favorite aunt, who had kept house for her widowed father, an Irish police sergeant, and brought up my mother, two other sisters, and a brother. To me, she was my second mother. Whatever small wisdom I have came from her. If she's not in heaven, I don't want to go there!

"Morris darlin'," she told me one day. "Never argue with the Irish! They're slippery as eels in a bucket, and they've always got God on their side! So don't buy into their squabbles. Button your lip, and walk away. You'll keep your dignity and save yourself a lot of heartache."

That took care of the Brother Superior, with whom I knew I couldn't win anyway. It didn't answer the larger question about Brother Avellino. He and I were supposed to be brothers in a community; we were supposed to be living under a common rule, but clearly a different set of rules was being applied to him. In my folly, I decided to confront him. I wasn't about to demand the return of my baton, only to ask his personal explanation of events.

Well now! Eels in a bucket, was it? Kerry horse-coper, was it? This was the great Daniel O'Connell himself, back from the dead, eloquent with righteous amazement. Had he not tended me and done my work every long day of my illness? Had he not held my hand and mopped my brow while I babbled in the fever? Had I not pleaded with him to take over the baton and conduct the choir in a triumphal marching chorus to victory? He smote me hip and thigh with singulars and plurals: "I said, you said, we agreed, and was it not so now? And for the sake of the boys that have put so much into this, should we not put an end to rivalry and confusion? Besides, I'm the senior and the more experienced and the better able to handle a public occasion. The Brother Superior himself recognized that."

My sainted aunt was right. There was nothing for it but to button my lip and walk away, wrapping the last rags of my dignity around me. Still, my trials weren't over. Every day Brother Avellino walked into my classroom for choir practice, while I was shunted into his domain, out of sight but not out of earshot of my singers. Every day he offered his brightest smile and a variation on the same bit of blarney: "You'll be keeping an ear cocked now, won't you? And if you hear anything that fails to please you, you'll let me know, won't you? They're still your boys. I try to make them feel that, and they do . . ." After a week of it, I gave up listening. After two, I was past caring. When the choir was eliminated in the first audition, I managed to find enough grace to tell the boys it was a good try and enough irony to offer tea and aspirin to Avellino, who was taken to his bed with a migraine.

The Brother Superior, however, went public with lavish praises of what he called Avellino's splendid effort under difficult circumstances. He pointed out that my compliance had saved me from the great disappointment that Avellino was bearing valiantly in my place. I felt like throwing up. Instead, I poured out my anger to the Senior Member.

"Why is he acting like this? The competition's over. We lost. Why does he have to keep on justifying Avellino?"

The Senior Member studied me over the steel rims of his spectacles. He keened over me like a mourning dove. He quoted the Apocrypha at me.

"'Weep for the dead one because he has been taken from the light. Weep for the fool because he has no understanding.' Where do you think you're living, boy? In Thomas More's Utopia? This is real life, the purgative way, and the sooner you wake up to it, the better. But as to your question, don't you know there's an election coming up?"

"What election? I haven't heard of one."

"Because you don't listen. You're so busy contemplating your own navel, you don't watch what's going on around you. These are elections to the provincial council, the governing body under which, believe it or not, you live!"

"I haven't seen a ballot paper."

"But you wouldn't, would you, because you're a junior under temporary vows and you don't have voting rights. That's the constitution you chose to live under, but obviously nobody's directed your attention to its meanings!"

"But what's this got to do with Avellino and the Brother Superior?"

"Give me strength! The Brother Superior's a candidate for election. His nomination is in, signed by Brother Avellino and some others. Now does it make sense?"

"Not quite. What does Avellino get out of it—and don't tell me it's a choirmaster's baton!"

"Not at all. He fancies himself as a musician, but he's got no talent for it. What he really wants is to be appointed a superior and run his own community. What quicker way to arrange it than to have a friend on the council?"

"That's despicable!" Even now, I can hear the outraged innocence in my voice. "Canvassing for oneself or another is forbidden by the rules!"

"Is it now? So, you're beginning to remember a few things! Sure it's forbidden, but that doesn't mean to say it's not practiced—under another name. The idea disgusts you?" The Senior Member nodded placidly. "But that's what happens when you want anything too much. You end up licking boots and backsides to get it. It's the way of the world, boy, and if you think the world isn't here inside our own walls, you're too damned innocent for your own good!"

And there it was, plain as the nose on my face—and I'd have seen it if I'd looked in a mirror. I was just as guilty as they were, just as ridiculous in my search for a juvenile satisfaction, redress for petty wrong.

In one particular, however, I was different—not better, just different: I had not attempted to use the mechanisms of power to procure my own satisfaction or subdue an adversary who threatened me. I had not used them, because I did not control them, as did the Brother Superior or, in his own degree, Brother Avellino. But the mechanisms existed. They could be used. They would be used. They had been used in my case.

As I look back now over a gap of sixty-two years, I see that moment as the beginning of the slow erosion of my convictions about the authenticity of my own vocation to religious life. For one thing, the life wasn't religious of itself, only insofar as its practitioners made it so. For another, my own innocence was spurious because it was untested. I was not a pilgrim in progress. I was a raw youth in flight from certain unpleasant realities in his life. I would not solve my problem by making other illusions out of other and harsher realities. It would take me a long and painful time to face the truth. At the end of that year, I applied for a transfer to a different community. The pilgrimage had just begun.

For a long time, I could not rid myself of the presence of Brother Avellino. I knew him, or thought I knew him, for a trivial man who could neither harm me nor help me, but, every now and then, on the faces of total strangers, I would see his dark gypsy eyes studying me, his easy horse-coper's smile flashing at me. Inside the monastic walls and, long afterward, outside them, his phantom presence was always associated with the same kind of experience. I would want something very badly—an assignment, a contract, an introduction. There would always be a horse-trader with Avellino's eyes and Avellino's smile waiting to procure it for me—for minimal consideration, out of pure friendship or professional respect. Always my hackles would rise, and I would become guarded and brusque. I wanted no bargains, just a fair deal at a fair market price, with no favors given and none owed. That was Avellino's legacy to me: a Homeric distrust of horse-traders. *Timeo Danaos et dona ferentes!*

I will not weary you, or myself, with the recitation of my next five years in the Congregation. I kept the vows I had made. I taught in small schools and large ones. I began my university studies as an external student, and later I took night courses at the University of Hobart. I taught English, Latin, French, chemistry, and mathematics and studied until the small hours of the morning in a tiny room next to a dormitory where fifty boarders slept. I trained a football team and umpired cricket matches and made the friendship of a lifetime with one Paddy Forrest—God rest his soul—who was a scholar and a gentle spirit and who deserved better than life or the Congregation offered him. We walked together through the town and the countryside of what was once the cruelest penal colony in the world, Van Diemen's Land (now Tasmania). He died while I was far away in England.

As far as my interior life was concerned, it was one of progressive alienation. I was uncomfortable in community life. I found small consolation in the rituals of religious observance. I became more and more critical of the hand-me-down philosophies by which our lives, and indeed our conversations, were limited.

I was then committed to temporary vows, binding for twelve months only. Each year one applied to renew the vows, and the application was judged on reports from one's immediate superior and senior members of the community. After ten years of temporary vows, one applied to make a final and perpetual commitment. I had already served seven years when I declined to renew my vows. The account of that decision, which I wrote during my army days, still holds good:

> "Return to the world." A queer little phrase, one of those archaic commonplaces of conventual literature and daily speech

that lose so quickly the burnish of their first coining; but for him, on this bright December morning, resting a space before stepping down into the crowd, quick with meaning and with promise.

Return to the world. From the white vigils on the hills, from the celibate service in the hidden shrine, return. Rip the fillets from the unwilling brow, spill out the wine and trample the cakes of offering underfoot. Turn your back on the stone of sacrifice, and with no backward, no regretful glance, go down to the valleys, to the town, to the people, to the laughter, and the singing, and the sorrow, and the hurry and the hate. Return—a free citizen. No questioning eyes now upon your sombre livery, no sense of segregation and of loss.

My exit from religious life was so discreet as to be almost furtive. That was the way of things in those far-off days. He who put his hand to the plow and looked back was deemed unfit for the Kingdom of Heaven. I was endowed with forty pounds in cash, a civilian suit, two changes of shirts and underwear, a hat and overcoat, and a second-class rail ticket to my hometown. My departure was timed for the hour when students and masters were in chapel. The Brother Provincial gave me a cool handshake and a reminder—somehow almost comic in the circumstances—that I was still under vows until their term expired at Christmas, which was six weeks away. My vows were to poverty, chastity, obedience, and perseverance in the Congregation. I was most certainly poor. I was no longer beholden to superiors, I was already halfway out the gate—and I surrendered my chastity to the first gesture of affection from a woman.

My homecoming was an embarrassment of welcome and tenderness from my widowed mother and my brothers and sisters. The sadness was that I did not know how to respond to it. My absence had been too long. My family ties had been too crudely cut. To use the jargon of a later time, I had been too thoroughly institutionalized. I had no name then for what ailed me, but I knew that I had to find the cure for myself. Within a matter of days, I had found myself a job serving in the men's haberdashery department of a well-known store that always hired temporary help for the Christmas season.

Though I say it myself, I was good at it. On bad days, I still console myself with the thought that if all else fails I can still go back to selling menswear! I can still knot a tie around my finger to display to a woman customer. I can still discuss the set of a shirt collar or the quality of hide in a pair of gloves. I learned to comport myself with passable comfort among my peers, the women and the men who made up the staff. I also learned to drink liquor and invite a girl out to a meal or a dance. It was a fast-track course, but it was no answer to the looming question of what I was going to do with the rest of my life and what real equipment I had to do it with.

This, I must remind you, was the tag-end of 1940. Sooner or later, I would have to join one of the armed services. However, what Saint Augustine told himself about chastity, I told myself about the war: "Not yet!" I wanted to live a little before I got myself killed.

So, when I was laid off from the store after Christmas, I spent my shop assistant's savings on a holiday at a seaside resort. During the holiday, I applied for a teaching post with the State Education Department. They handed it to me on a silver dish. Already the armed forces were draining away male staff.

So, there you have me in February of 1941: a teacher in a small country town, boarding in a small country pub, spending most of my cash on weekend trips to the big city to see a woman I had met on holiday, and nursing a new guilt. While Australian troops were taking heavy casualties in the North African desert, I was still a dominie in a classroom. The only change from my previous estate was that I was wearing a tie instead of a Roman collar. You should understand, given the reactionary nature of my Irish Catholic training, I had only a rudimentary sense of national identity. However, I embraced it eagerly as much from personal need as from intellectual conviction. I was still trying to assemble the elements of my fragmented identity.

Midway through the first school term, I called in sick. Acting on pure impulse and a vast unreason, I marched myself into Army Headquarters and asked to see the director of military intelligence. It was then exactly what it looks to me now: an act of megalomanic folly. I am still amazed by the outcome. The D.M.I. consented to see me. He asked me what he could do for me. I told him, haltingly, that the question was rather whether I had anything of use to him. I must have been an odd enough specimen to interest him. He invited me to explain.

I told him of my curious life and of my rather special education. I also told him one of the ways in which I, as a celibate religious, had used my spare time. For twenty minutes each day, I had forced myself to study a foreign language. By the time I quit the Congregation I was competent in half a dozen European languages and adequate in a few more odd ones. I could recite the Provençal poems of Mistral. I could read a newspaper in Romanian and piece out a text in Swedish.

The director was impressed. I am impressed now by my youthful gall and by how much I have forgotten in fifty-five years. The director called in an aide to run me through some elementary tests in German, Italian, and French. Then he ordered me to report for enlistment in seven days. I would do six weeks' basic military training in a country camp. After that, I would be posted with sergeant's rank to the Headquarters' cipher office. It was, I confess, a moment of pure joy. It added one more small piece to the defaced mosaic of myself.

After my experience as a novice, the disciplines of army training were a cakewalk to me. I was no great soldier, but I did what I was told and kept my mouth shut. I was in good physical condition. I worked out some of my frustrations at bayonet drill and in unarmed combat. I became a passable marksman with pistol and rifle. Socially, I was, perforce, more a listener than a talker. There was more than a decade of my life that I could neither explain nor share, because there was scant sympathy for scholarship or religious reminiscence in a rookie camp. It took me some time to learn the vocabulary of an Australian infantryman—in which, later, I became quite eloquent.

When I reported back to Headquarters with my sergeant's stripes up, I was told I could live outside barracks and be paid a subsistence allowance. So I spent the first months of my war behind the locked doors of a cipher room and my free time enjoying a love affair in suburbia.

Such experience brought its own new confinement and its own sense of unreality. I could not discuss the work I did. My loving was too new and special to be shared either! I had a worm's-eye view of universal cataclysm and a fool's faith in the magic rituals of love.

Toward the end of that year, volunteers were called from our section to serve in the Independent Companies that were being formed to establish themselves in Timor, Ambon, and other islands of what were then known as the Dutch East Indies. I was among the three chosen. We were told to sit tight and wait for posting orders. Meantime, we were promoted to the rank of lieutenant.

That meant, of course, a raise in pay and family allowances. It seemed a good idea to get married. We were churched and blessed, according to the rites of the Roman Catholic Church, and we lived together in a fair copy of domestic contentment until Pearl Harbor was attacked and Singapore fell, and the

Japanese bombed the northern Australian city of Darwin. The city was evacuated. I was ordered north as part of a military contingent to restore essential communication services. All the news was bad. Fourteen Allied warships had been sunk in the Java Sea. Java itself had surrendered. The best of our fighting men were away in North Africa fighting with the British. General Douglas MacArthur arrived from the Philippines and was appointed commander in chief of Allied forces in the Pacific. We had a general, but we had precious little else.

I flew from Adelaide to Darwin in a creaking DC-3. It was my first flight, and I was constantly airsick from the buffeting we took at low altitudes. I was so sick that they off-loaded me at Newcastle Waters, where the Royal Australian Air Force had a small station. My hosts fed me warm beer and curried mince and stale bread, which did nothing at all to ease my spasms. I was still queasy when, next morning, they loaded me into another DC-3 and flew me into Darwin.

It was a ghost town then. The small population of civilian officials, Chinese merchants, road gangers, local residents, cattlemen, and prisoners from Fanny Bay jail had all fled. The few luggers, relics of the pearling days, lay careened on the tide flats. The Timor Sea stretched gray and oily under the monsoon clouds. The airport was a shambles, pitted with bomb craters, littered with burned-out aircraft, its hangars gutted and gaping. Its only inhabitants were a small air force detachment with no planes to fly and a few civil aviation officials. I told them I was posted to the Twenty-one Mile, where might that be? They shrugged and pointed to a telephone that, with luck, might connect me with the camp. I waited for three hours until a bored-looking driver arrived with a half-ton truck, slung my gear on board, and pointed us southward down The Bitumen.

I slept that night in a sodden tent, pitched between pandanus palms, with the kangaroo grass growing three feet above my head. The rain sheeted down all night; a myriad moths and mosquitoes fluttered around the kerosene lamp; a mantis, long as my hand, perched on my pillow. I woke at midnight to the howling of dingoes and the creaking of the jungle under-growth.

It was a strange time, an eerie time. The Japanese were expected to invade the Australian mainland. We had no idea where they would strike. The whole of northern Australia was encircled. Every unit was on watch for enemy infiltrators. Hostile spotter planes were over every day. Sometimes they dropped a few bombs; most times they didn't. The mangrove swamps were silent and sinister. The jungle fringe was full of mystery for a raw, young lieutenant bred in the temperate south. It took a little time to grasp the fact that this was my first command. Men's lives, and a lot of military secrets, were in my hands. I began to grow up.

Dimly at first, then with increasing conviction, I understood that I had, somehow, to come to terms with the past I could not share. There were few diversions at the Twenty-one Mile. So, using a battered orderly room typewriter and the backs of army message pads, I began to write a book.

I carted the manuscript pages with me for nearly two years. I scrawled them during convoy bivouacs. I pored over them in the long night hours on signal watch, and, finally, when I came to Mount Isa in the far northwest of Queensland, I found a woman to type them. She was employed at the huge mine site as a secretary, but once she had been a secretary to a famous American author, Zane Grey.

As her pile of typescript grew, I carried it back to our camp in the saddlebags of my dispatch rider's motorcycle. I piled it up on the table in my tent with a stone on top of it. I would gloat over it before I went to sleep. Then, one day, a desert whirlwind blew through the open tent and the precious pages were scattered over a square mile of stony landscape where feral goats cropped the sparse saltbush.

Panic-stricken, I drove about the encampment trying to recover the pages. Of more than two hundred fifty pages, I recovered something less than a hundred. I had to begin again to fill in the gaps. So never talk to me about Sir Isaac Newton or Thomas Carlyle and the disasters that happened to their manuscripts!

I finished the book in a panicked rush. I signed it with the pseudonym Julian Morris, because, although it was couched in the form of fiction, it was, for the most part, an accurate record of my experiences as a Christian Brother. I gave it the title *Moon in My Pocket,* which is the last line of Robert Browning's poem *Master Hugues of Saxe-Gotha.* When it was published in 1943 it became a minor *succès de scandale.* It sold ten thousand copies, which, in wartime Australia, was a minor miracle.

Looking at it now, I feel no pride in it. It was the book of a very young man, full of self-pity and romantic hopes. I have never sought to republish it. Its account of my life and religion was accurate, but it carried an artificially happy ending that later events inevitably belied. Still, it was a landmark event in my life. It led to my exit from the army and my first employment in politics. In hindsight, it marked, too, the beginning of the end of my first marriage.

I make the comment without cynicism. The marriage turned out to be a sad mistake for both of us. It lasted longer than it should have because I was absent for three years of it, and when I came home, we were strangers—which is worse than being enemies. There is a terrible oppression about slow estrangement, and when it is compounded by the canonical prescriptions of a church, the oppression becomes intolerable and, in the end, a destructive tyranny. The sadness was that neither of us could relearn the lessons of love, because our union was flawed by a silly lie, that, once revealed, I could not forget—had not grace enough to live with, nor love enough to endure.

There were reasons for that, too, but they are no part of this testimony. Some of them are buried forever in the files of the Rota. I gave no evidence in the divorce that followed our separation. My first wife is dead these many years. There is a bond of love between myself and the children we had together.

I have been asked many times whether my departure from the Congregation triggered an exit from the Church. My answer is plain: I never left the Church. I stayed always within it as a professing and confessing member, even when I was under sentence of ipso facto excommunication. My claim was always—and time and providence have justified it—that my membership in the Church was a birthright conferred by baptism, and no one had the right to expel me from it, especially for unjust cause. I claim no special virtue in my stance. It was simply a repeated affirmation of what I have always believed: that I was and am a legitimate inheritor of the Christian message and of the brotherhood and sisterhood of the faithful. I was and am a member of the family. I have stood always upon my right to remain within it.

This, I believe, is the meaning of the metaphor with which I began this book. *A View from the Ridge* reveals an extraordinary unity. The pieces of a huge jigsaw have fitted themselves into place. I have been led to the place of contemplation. I cannot see the hand that guided me; nonetheless, I perceive it to be there and I have been grateful for its saving touch.

CHAPTER 3

KEEPERS
of the DREAMING

My sojourn at the Twenty-one Mile was short. My section was shifted two hundred miles south to the Northern Territory town of Katherine, a place that is now a major tourist resort, but that, in those days, had a whistle-stop railway station, one pub, a slaughterhouse where cattle were butchered for army supplies, and a large military hospital that was to serve as a forward base hospital in the event of invasion. There were also major units of engineers, signals, transport, and supply and a base for civilian engineers building the highway.

The road southward from Darwin was slowly being turned from bull dust to bitumen, and more and more convoys were rolling northward with supplies. Many of the convoys were run by U.S. transport units manned by black troops and commanded by southern white officers. I rode with them many times, and when, in my third year, I was shifted across the continent from Katherine to the Queensland mining town of Mount Isa, I saw a black man shot by a white officer because he had approached an Australian girl to ask her for a dance. It was my first experience with racist murder.

I had other assignments, too. In Katherine I made my first contact with our indigenous Aboriginal people—the Jawoyn, who were the traditional owners of the land and the owners of their own language. Their ancestors had created the huge rock paintings in the gorges of the Katherine River, which are one of the wonders of the area. I knew nothing of their history. I used some of the men as trackers and scouts to report any traces of Japanese infiltration, but I had no means of entering their private lives. I would sit by their campfires, listening to their chants and trying, without success, to find some key to their murmured conversation.

It was only in later years that I began to learn their cosmology and their legends. It was later still that I understood how much we have to learn from them about our own relationship with our huge but fragile country and the threatened ecology of our planet.

My contacts with them had, however, a curious aftermath. Many years later, in 1986 to be exact, Pope John Paul II made his first official visit to Australia. I received a telephone call from a man I had never met: the parish priest of Alice Springs, which is now a thriving tourist town and the capital of the Red Heart of the continent. He asked me whether I would be willing to come, with my wife, and help him to prepare the town for the papal visit.

The request made no sense to me at all. I didn't belong there. I would be inevitably regarded as an intruder, and a presumptuous one at that.

The parish priest persisted; I did know the territory. I had written a novel about it, *The Naked Country,* that had later been filmed. I had more personal and professional authority than I realized. I asked him what he expected me to do or say. He was vague about that. He was very precise about other matters. In spite of its rapid growth and its real prosperity, the town was in a constant state of tension. There was a large community of detribalized Aboriginal people—fringe dwellers who had fallen victim to the white man's curse of alcohol. There was a small, permanent community of white people who had vested interests in the town. There was another community of workers from outlying cattle stations and local service industries. There was a casino in the town but precious little else by way of relaxation. Alcohol consumption was high. Brawls and fights were common. A government paper had been prepared on the real possibilities of civil disorder.

There were religious divisions, too. The first missions in the area were Lutheran. Then the Catholics came and the Anglicans and all the other religious groups. Rivalries, small and large, simmered between them. The parish priest hoped that the forthcoming papal visit would provide a focus for some kind of unity. I told him, bluntly, that it could equally foment dissension and prejudice. He was a persistent man. He argued his case stubbornly. Finally, we compromised.

I would fly out to see him with my wife and at my own expense. If I could see a good purpose in my intervention, I would stay. If not, I would leave. He agreed. He would pick us up from the airport, and we would spend two nights as guests in his presbytery.

The first day he took us on a tour of the town. We had been there as tourists. I had been there during the war because "the Alice" was the beginning and the end of the convoy run to Darwin. The town he showed us was a different place altogether. He took us first to see the fringe dwellers, the Aboriginal communities living in government-supplied housing on the edges of the town. He showed me how the men spent their idle days in traditional meeting places in the dry bed of the river, where their middens were everywhere visible: piles of beer cans and broken bottles. It was a depressing sight, and, once again, I put the question to the priest and to myself: "What can I say that will make any sense to or about these lost people?"

That same evening, he invited us to attend a meeting in the presbytery. The participants were women from the fringe-dwelling communities. It was in them that the true strength of the Aboriginal people still resided. Their fear was for the children. The men were living on dole money, most of which was spent on liquor. The women, however, still hoped and argued and fought, sometimes physically, for the well-being of the children. Late in the evening, two or three men drifted in to the meeting. They had obviously been drinking and were very much the worse for wear. The women berated them publicly. They apologized for their conduct. As a spectator male, I felt ashamed for them. I was becoming more and more sure that there was no place for me in this argument.

I could not see much for the pope either. I could not see much point in the formal speeches that would be prepared for him and that he would deliver in his heavy accent from the altar that was being constructed at the racecourse. I could not see the relevance of that ritual to the brute quality of life in the Red Center. I could not imagine how anything I might say or do would make any sense either.

When the meeting was over, my wife, Joy, stayed to have tea with the women. The parish priest walked me over to the schoolhouse in the adjoining block. There was someone he wanted me to meet. The someone was a tall, white-haired Aborigine working on a huge canvas that was to be the backdrop for the altar at the papal mass. It was a traditional dot painting in the earth colors of the region. I asked the painter to explain it to me. He did so haltingly because his people are shy with white strangers—and they have good reason to be. He told me that the painting represented a tribal history of the Aranda people, their sacred places, their totem animals, their whole cosmogony of creation, the land that owned them, and the magical beings who had created its hills and hollows and the gorges where the precious secret waters lay.

I thanked him for his time and for the trouble he had taken with me. The parish priest and I walked out into a velvet darkness under a sky full of stars that looked so close one had only to reach up and pluck one.

"That man," said the priest abruptly, "is a very special person. He is the Keeper of the Dreaming for all his people. They have no written language. All their history is orally transmitted. All of it is locked inside the head of that man. The sadness is that as the young men drift away from the outlying tribes, they are lost and their history is lost, too. Out in the hills there," he gestured vaguely toward the black ridges of the Macdonnell Ranges, "out there in the hills, there is a tribal group that calls itself the Painted Men. They are trying to re-form their tribal life. They come into town and kidnap the young bucks and take them away into the hills and force them to undergo the ceremonies of tribal initiation. They believe that this is the only way to restore their tribe and preserve the foundations of tribal life. I cannot tell you much more about them because it's not white man's business, but I do see the point of it, and I do see the importance of that old man back in the schoolroom."

Quite suddenly, I saw it, too. The man who was coming, the Pope of Rome, was also the Keeper of a Dreaming. His dreaming, however, was only two thousand years old. The dreaming of these people went back at least forty thousand years and possibly even longer. Was any union, was any understanding, even possible?

I spent a restless night with that question buzzing around in my head. In the morning, after breakfast, I tried out the idea on the parish priest. I suggested we spend that day visiting other groups in the community: church groups, teachers, traders, to try on them the text "The Keeper of the Dreaming." If it made sense to them, if it touched a chord of understanding, then I would consent to write and speak about the papal visit. If it didn't, then my thinking and my feeling were too far astray to be useful.

The visits we made that day and the talks we had with a variety of people have lingered in my memory. Not all their responses were immediate. Most of them, however, were positive. They understood the need for reconciliation, for the building of bridges. They understood that somehow they, too, had to throw off the burden of their own history and make a new beginning. They all agreed: the symbol of a Dreamtime was a foundation on which they could build. They grasped readily the notion that while our symbols—personal, national, or tribal—were not identical, they did express a truth common to us all: We issue from a mystery and we depart into a mystery. If we wish to live peacefully between the beginning and the end, we have each to receive from the others the gift of whatever understanding they can offer.

I have found all through my life a connection—even a concordance—between the events of my past and the events of a distant and, seemingly, improbable future. During my posting in Katherine, I spent much time with one of my sergeants, experienced in bushcraft, exploring the reaches of the river and the timberlands and the savanna that fringed it. I remember one day coming upon a timber platform raised high above the kangaroo grass. On the platform was laid the body of an Aboriginal man who had obviously been dead for some time. The eagles and the carrion birds were circling above it. The stones below the platform were splashed with the fluids of decomposition and the feces of the carrion birds. The corpse would lie there until it was reduced to a skeleton. Then, it would be taken down and dismembered. The bones would be packed into a hollow tube made from a pandanus log, which would be painted with ocher and then lodged in a secret place. When this ceremony was completed, the spirits of the dead would be at rest and would not haunt the lives of the living.

One day, my companion and I discovered such a burial place. It looked at first like a hole in the ground between the roots of a great ficus tree. The following day, we went down into the hole with torches. We found that the air was fresh and clean and that we were in the first of a series of chambers receding and narrowing into the distance. The floor was dry sand, the channel of an underground river that in flood time would be a torrent. In the recesses and cavities of the rock walls were hollowed logs containing the bones of the dead. There were weapons with them and small painted sticks whose meanings were hidden from us. It was not a sinister place. There was a curious neutrality about it—the same neutrality that I experienced many years later in Rome when I first visited the catacombs of San Callisto on the Appian Way. There, too, I was confronted by the mystery of our human sameness and the differences of time, custom, and belief that turned us into enemies.

I remember very vividly the impression produced on me by two signs on the old funerary road. One, impressive and monumental, marked the entrance to the Christian catacombs. The other was a plain wooden notice board defaced by time and weather that stood at the entrance to the closed gate of a vineyard. The sign read simply: *Catacombe degli Ebraei*—The Catacombs of the Jews. It was a reminder that even here, among the dead, anti-Semitism prevailed. In olden times, the burial places of the Jewish community were contiguous to and, in some cases, continuous with the Christian ones.

A mile away, on the Via Ardeatina, was a national monument to the three hundred hostages, some of them Jews, some of them Gentiles, who were rounded up by the Germans after a partisan raid on the officers' brothel on the Via Rasella in Rome. Thirty officers were killed in that raid. Three hundred hostages, ten for one, were rounded up and machine-gunned inside the tufa caverns of the Fossa Ardeatina. The caverns were then blown up to blot out the crime. After the war, the victims were exhumed and reburied at the place of execution, which is now a national shrine. How and by what strange trick of memory—or is it a process of revelation—do these memories connect themselves in my mind? The older I get, the more convinced I am that every human life is an evolutionary process during which the Creator offers to the creature an experience of divinity, an opportunity, great or small, to share in the ongoing act of creation. I find it hard to express that conviction, because language itself is so limited. For example, the only way in which I have been able to come to terms with a violent creation—which is how, sooner or later, the majority of humankind experiences it—is to regard it not as a complete act but as an ongoing process evolving toward a final triumphant conclusion in which even the casualties and the horrors and the terrible paradoxes will make a divine sense.

I cannot prove any of this. I lack the language and the will even to debate it. I hold it, if you like, as a pilgrim hope when night falls and the terrors of the road seem to draw closer. Years ago, I tried to express it in my novel *The Clowns of God,* in which there appeared a series of letters to God written by a deposed pope under the pseudonym "Johnny the Clown." In simple modern form they recalled the Old Testament disputations between man and God. They were intended also to recall the final terrible question of the crucified Jesus: "My God, my God, why have you forsaken me?" Here is part of one of the letters of Johnny the Clown:

Dear God,

If You're the beginning and the end of it all, why didn't You give us all an equal chance? In a circus, You know, our lives depend on that. If the riggers make a mistake, the trapeze artists die. If the man with the thunderflash doesn't do it right, I lose my eyes.

But, You don't seem to look at things that way. A circus travels, so we get to see how other people live—and I mean good people who love each other and love their children and really deserve a pat on the head from You.

Now, here's the thing I can't understand. You know it all. You made it all. But everyone sees You differently. You've even let Your children kill each other; just because they each have a different description of Your face at the window! . . . Why do we all use different marks to tell us we're Your children? I was sprinkled with water because my parents were Christians. Louis, the lion tamer, had a little piece cut off his penis because he's a Jew. Leila, the black girl who handles the snakes, wears an ammonite around her neck, because this is the magical snakestone. . . . And yet, when the show is over and we all sit at the supper table, tired and hungry, do You see much difference between us? Do you care? Are you really very upset when Louis, who is getting old and scared, creeps into Leila's bed for a little comfort, and Leila, who is really quite ugly, is glad to have him?

I seem to remember that Your Son enjoyed eating and drinking and chatting with people like us. He liked children. He seemed to understand women. It's a pity nobody bothered to record very much of his talk with them—a few words with his mother, the rest was mostly with girls who were on the town, one way and another.

What I'm trying to say is that You're shutting down the world without really giving us a chance to overcome the handicaps You've given us . . . I have to say that. I wouldn't be honest if I let the matter pass. Somewhere up near the North Pole there's an old woman sitting on an ice floe. She's not suffering. She's fading slowly away. Her family have put her there. She's content, because this is the way death has always been arranged for the old. You know she's there. I'm sure You're making it easy—more easy perhaps than for some other poor old dear in a very expensive clinic. But You've never told us very clearly which situation You prefer. I like to believe it's the one with the more loving in it!

I never thought to ask before. Can you, God, change Your mind? If not, why not? And if You can, why didn't You do it before we all got into such a terrible mess? I'm sorry if I sound rude. I don't mean to be.

Some years ago, I embarked on an ambitious project, a history of the Roman papacy for worldwide television. The first episode had been made and distributed when I had to undergo cardiac surgery. There was no way I could face the rest of the project. I abandoned it. However, one small episode sticks in my mind.

We were filming at Castel Gandolfo, which is the summer residence of the popes. It is also the site of the Vatican Observatory and the bailiwick of the papal astronomer, a very bright American Jesuit whose name is George Coyne. He is an astrophysicist of world renown and spends most of his time in Phoenix, Arizona. When I asked him what he did in Rome, he explained, with a grin, that he came each year "to polish the lenses of the telescope and present a paper at the Academy." I discovered later that he had involved the Vatican in a current worldwide experiment to determine the possibility of life forms on other celestial bodies. I reminded him that this precisely was one of the heretical theses for which Giordano Bruno had been condemned and burned. He made a wry mouth and said, "I know. Funny, isn't it?"

We were installed with our camera crew inside the observatory tower itself. The tower dominated the gardens, where, at that precise moment, Pope John Paul II was walking up and down, reciting his breviary. We were under strict orders not to intrude in any fashion upon his sacred privacy. I began to walk the papal astronomer through our interview. I asked him first how much of the heavens he could see from Castel Gandolfo. He shrugged and said, "Not much. The smog's too thick."

My next question was a metaphysical one: "You deal with astrophysics and phenomena. You deal with extensions and distances beyond our capacity to grasp. What does your science tell you about God?"

He shrugged again and said, "Not much more than you can learn from a leaf or a pinch of dust. There's more of it. The diversity and the extension run off the scale, but the mysteries of creation and the Creator still remain."

I asked him then, "What does creation tell you about the soul?"

Once again he answered with an evasion.

"I have to tell you, Morris, I have always been bothered about the soul."

I knew what he meant: the old dualist notion of spirit and matter, of soul and body, was inadequate to express the mysterious unity of the human person and of the person with the cosmos itself. I put to him a third question, this one off the record. I gestured toward the garden where the pope was still pacing and reciting his breviary. I asked, "How would the pope answer the question I have just asked you?"

He spread his hands in a dismissive gesture: "As pope he would probably decline to debate the question with you. He is elected to govern a universal church, to hold fast to the primal deposit of faith, and to confirm the moralities of Christian life. In that office he cannot afford the luxury of public speculation. That's where you and I, my friend, are lucky."

When I was a schoolboy, and later still when I was in training as a religious, the doctrine of the Fall and the doctrine of redemption were always expressed as "an infinite offense to an infinite being, an offense that could be purged only by the redemptive act of the life and death of Jesus Christ, the son of God himself."

I have always had a problem with that theology. It is my personal experience that the noblest and the worst human beings are incapable of infinities. The greatest horrors in history are still limited events. Six million victims of the Holocaust, twenty million war casualties—these are still finite figures.

It is for this reason that I find I cannot believe in the fundamentalist idea of eternal and, therefore, infinite punishment for a finite act. I cannot accept the Creator in the role of torturer, nor can I find any joy in contemplation of the suffering of others. Extinction or exclusion from beatitude I can understand, however dimly. Reward and punishment are, however, human terms in which we express our belief—or at least our hope—in the final cosmic balance of things, the divine rationality of a creative plan that human reason cannot compass.

There is a deeper mystery still: the infinite goodness of an infinite God, which I believe in spite of all the evidence against it.

For the Christian, there is the promise "to restore all things in Christ." How or when that restoration may be accomplished, I do not know. I wait unknowing with the rest of the human family.

CHAPTER 4

ENCOUNTERS

L et me explain something to you. The mindscape lies outside the geography of normal life. Its elements and its images are authentic, but they seem at first glance unreal, disconnected, like figures in a surrealist canvas. The light has a noonday brightness but an arctic chill. The shadows it throws are sharp, but its reflections produce sometimes a dazzlement or a confusion. I tell you openly, therefore, that what I think I see may not be exactly what is or what was then. As old Ben Jonson said long ago, "Memory, of all the powers of the mind, is the most delicate and frail." So, if memory fails me sometimes, I beg you not to name me a liar, but put it down to a trick of the light and the impairments of age.

I remember myself, a youth still in my teens, dressed in a black cassock and stretched prone on a marble pavement vowing poverty, chastity, obedience, and perseverance in the service of God.

I remember myself, a much older man, in the season that is called maples-in-flame, standing beside the pool in the monastery of Tenryu-ji while the Zen master presented me with the riddles that bend the mind out of logic and into perception:

"Only when one is free from words can one really understand words."

"One in all, all in one. Only when this is understood will you cease to worry about imperfections."

In another exotic context, I recall Jim Thompson, the Silk King of Thailand, dining in his ancient teak house, preening himself for his distinguished guests while the parrot on his shoulder fed from his fork and then walked along the table pecking at the bosoms of the women while Jim Thompson looked on and chuckled. He was a handsome and beguiling man, but he had been drilled in the secret and soulless trade of military intelligence and there was a streak of perversity and cruelty in him also. He disappeared off the planet in upland Malaya, and sedulous legends were spun about the unsolved mystery.

Then there was the Feather Man, my friend Keith Hyland, with factories in Bangkok and Saigon. He was the master of a whole army of cyclists throughout the deltas who brought him duck feathers and military intelligence, and his life was more mysterious than his death. During the Tet offensive in Vietnam, he was taken prisoner in Cholon by a unit of the Vietcong. For most of his captivity he was held in a deep pit. He was starved and humiliated, but he managed to hold himself together and maintain his personal dignity and the respect of his captors. I have in my possession some of the records of his debriefing session after his release. None of them gives a complete picture of a complex and still mysterious man, whom all of his friends liked and none ever managed to record fully. I tried to persuade him to set down at least the outline of his life and experience as a wealthy exile in Thailand. He always refused.

I have a comic vision of the Fat Man in a black coat and striped trousers who tracked every visitor through the anterooms of the papal apartments in the Vatican. My first encounter with him was in the mid-fifties during an audience with His Holiness Pope Pius XII. We were half a dozen privileged visitors led through the papal anterooms by Vatican prelates, followed by the Fat Man, who walked always with his hands clasped under the tails of his coat. None of us knew who he was or what he did until the final moment, when he whipped the camera from under the tails of his coat and took photographs of our privileged group. It was just before the end of the audience that he came into his own. He marshaled us around the pope and even directed that august personage with serene authority. His name was Felici. He had a small shopfront on the Via del Babuino. He also had a hugely profitable monopoly on all photographs taken in, or issued from, Vatican City. After His Holiness had retired, he presented us with the simple question, "How many copies would you like? They cost six thousand lire apiece."

I have a vivid memory of a producer in Hollywood who conducted his conferences with a certain degree of high drama. He sat behind an enormous desk, in front of which was set one solitary chair with others ranged behind it at a respectful distance. The solitary chair was for the victim of the day. When you sat in it, you faced the great man across an acre of desktop.

Ranged on the outer edge of it, with their blades pointing toward you, was an array of killing knives of all shapes and sizes, meticulously oiled and polished. Behind the knives was the small stack of pages that you had delivered in the preceding few days. The producer's fair, white hands lay on either side of them. He never gave them more than a sidelong glance. If he deigned to touch them, it was always with an expression of extreme distaste. His preamble never varied.

"Well, I've read your stuff . . ."

You'd learned by now never to ask whether he liked it. He never did. So you sat silent. Then, inevitable as doom, came the grabber.

"Tell me; what's the sexiest love passage you've ever seen on the screen?"

Again, a well-trained beast, you sat silent and waited. Then the great man told you.

"A woman shaving a man . . . in bed!"

The visions conjured up were extraordinary. He hadn't said what part she was supposed to be shaving. I, being a writer, was instantly enmeshed in a wilderness of sexual fantasies, from the sublime to the quite ridiculous. He, being a producer, had no sense of the ridiculous, but he did have the power to read the minds of dumb beasts, and writers. He was shocked at what was going on in mine.

"You think it's dirty! I'm talking about his face . . ."

Now he was standing behind me, stroking my shoulders with the blade of the knife while he described in detail, shot by shot, how the scene would be recorded on film . . . her delicate fingers wiping away the soap from his mouth, her ruby lips seeking his as though through bubbles of sea foam . . . and so on, and so on, *ad nauseam*. Finally came the ritual question: "Do you think you can write it?"

I was sure the blade was near my jugular, but, courageous as a virgin martyr, I answered, "No, I think it stinks."

He was hurt and angry. It was as if I had insulted his manhood.

"Well, what's your idea of a sexy scene? Because this crap you've given me isn't sexy at all!"

You see how it works? It's a catch-22. Either you confirm the monster in his folly, or you commit yourself to a logic of madness by which the moon has to be made of green cheese, inhabited by witchetty grubs sent by rocket ship from the Red Center of Australia.

At this point, I must make a leap in time to introduce you to the pope's sister. She, of course, belonged in another country, and besides, to my certain knowledge, the wench is dead. However, her tale is worth telling.

It belongs to the mid-sixties, when I was in Rome working on the script of *The Shoes of the Fisherman*. You remember the book: the first Slavic pope . . . how, just released from prison in Russia, he was elected to the See of Peter? You remember his nighttime walk through the darkened city to see the true face of his people? Great, heady, dramatic stuff!—and we were working on it in Rome.

My producer on this one was the most agreeable of men. You couldn't offend him, you couldn't be offended by him. He was handsome, witty, charming, a schlepper to top all schleppers. We had fun on everything except the script. We dined often together at Romolo's in Trastevere. We drank Frascati wine. We sat late listening to our favorite *chitarrista* playing Neapolitan songs. We bought, for sweet charity, a rose from the elderly White Russian lady who always came in at eleven o'clock, sang one verse of "Dark Eyes," and then peddled her wilting blooms among the diners.

It was on one such evening that my producer challenged me with the "great idea."

"Morris, try this for size . . ."

It was late. I was full of wine, music, and benevolence. I walked straight into the snare.

"George, for this money, in Rome, in spring, for you, my friend, I'll try anything!"

"Morris, what if the pope had a sister?"

I had no argument with the proposition. Popes had mothers. They had fathers, uncles, aunts. Some had mistresses and bred children from them whom they called nephews and nieces. Clearly, they could run to a sister. So far, I had nothing to argue about. I simply asked, "So, the pope has a sister. Fine! What do we do with her?"

"That big scene, Morris, the one that's going to make or break the picture: the pope's nighttime walk through Rome. Are you with me?"

I was with him. I'd been with him for months and months and months, every step of the way. I would not falter now.

"I'm fascinated, George. Please tell me more."

"So, suppose, Morris . . . suppose, as Pope Kiril is walking through the low quarter of Rome, one of the prostitutes who accosts him on page fifty-six is a woman he recognizes, somebody lost to him from the war years. Suppose she is . . . *the pope's sister!*"

I swear to you it happened. I have only the haziest recollection of my reaction. I seem to remember that I drank myself silly for the rest of the evening. I seem to remember standing in the roof garden of the Cavalieri Hilton at three in the morning, wondering if it would hurt too much if I jumped!

I'm glad I didn't, because that would have destroyed the glamorous memory of Noel Coward and Lynn Fontanne tripping arm in arm down Schubert Alley in New York on the night my play *Daughter of Silence* opened to splendid reviews and to a week-long blizzard that closed us down.

I remember other, and grimmer, lanes in Naples where the scurrying urchins were called *scugnizzi*, spinning tops. It was there I met Mario Borrelli, the urchin priest, who shared their squalid lives and then, like the Pied Piper, led them into an abandoned church that became the legendary House of the Urchins. One of the best things I have done in my life was to tell his story to the world in a book called *Children of the Sun*. The book is still in print, and the House of the Urchins is still open. Borrelli and his work are still alive.

Children of the Sun was published in 1957. Two years later, in 1959, I published *The Devil's Advocate*, which became, in the jargon of the marketplace, a blockbuster. It was published in many languages. It won many prizes. It earned several million dollars, and it is still selling today. A year later, I was living in California. I was involved in weekly discussions on the stage version of the book, which later went to Broadway. *Daughter of Silence* was written, delivered, and predicted as another big best-seller. In short, I was the perfect model of the successful author. My mistakes and my failures were buried in the avalanche of praise.

Then, one fine day, I found myself in hospital, seriously ill. The heady vapors of success dissipated very quickly, like mist on the morning sea. Whatever I had won might soon be taken away from me. It would be a legacy to others but certainly no profit to me. Resentments vanished, too. There was no room for them in what might remain of my life. Every day brought me the most unexpected charities in the form of letters from readers who had heard of my illness through the press and were eager to tell me of what I had given to them through what I had written.

The most poignant of these letters was nearly thirty pages of beautiful calligraphy. It was from a young Jewish woman in California. It told how her family had fled from Germany to Spain after Kristallnacht. From Spain they had sought to emigrate to the United States. They were advised that if they were prepared to convert to Catholicism, they would be eligible for assistance from a church organization. The parents decided that a visa to the United States was certainly "worth a mass." The whole family was instructed and baptized into the Church.

My correspondent described to me her own very special situation. Suddenly, there was no threat in her life. She had a new, serene existence. She was at ease in her adopted identity. She described her joy at wearing her white first communion dress, her companionship with little girls of her own age. She had no knowledge—how could she?—of the repetitive ironies of Spanish history.

Finally, the family managed to obtain visas to the United States and, eventually, a permanent residence and citizenship. This done, all the family—except my correspondent—reverted to Judaism. As she explained it, she was happy being who and what she had become. The happiness lasted until she fell in love with a Jewish boy and had to ask the permission of her Catholic pastor to marry him! The pastor, in the fashion of the time, was less than understanding, and far less than sympathetic. In the end, she did marry her Jewish boy—and immediately fell under the crushing weight of a double guilt. She had secured her first freedom by abandoning her own people. She was now abandoning the people with whom she had found a first fragile security. The images of the Holocaust became her nightmares.

These profound conflicts within herself plunged her into deep clinical depression and brought her several times to the edge of suicide. She described the strange moment when she picked up *The Devil's Advocate* and began to read it. The dialogue between Aldo Meyer, the Jew in exile in his own country, and Monsignor Blaise Meredith, the ailing Vatican official, each loaded with his own private guilts, touched her deeply and brought meaning and hope back into her life.

Her letter gave me an extraordinary consciousness of continuity. I, too, was facing a possible termination, but what I had written was continuing to animate the lives of other people whom I had never met and never would meet.

Some years later, I wrote to this woman and asked her permission to incorporate part of the story she had told me into the book I was then writing, *The Shoes of the Fisherman*. She gave me the permission, and she is enshrined in the novel in the character of Ruth Lewin. When the book was published in America, I went back there for the launch. As I was signing copies in Brentwood Market, Los Angeles, a woman asked me to autograph the copy she had just bought. I asked the standard question: "How would you like it inscribed?" The name she gave me brought me half out of my chair. She laid a hand on my shoulder and forced me to sit again. She said, "Don't get up, don't say anything. I just wanted to thank you in person." Then she walked away and was lost in the crowd. I have never seen or heard from her again.

There were, by contrast, more sinister encounters: the dockside moneychanger in Beirut who became the biggest banker in the Middle East and entertained the desert chiefs in a silken tent in his boardroom where they could see their gold piled up under the canopy. I met him because I carried a letter of introduction from friends in Rome. I put him in a book, too, *The Tower of Babel*. He spent lavishly, invested all around the world. His enemies waited until he was less than 3 percent liquid, then pressed the panic button and laughed when his depositors withdrew their funds in a gadarene rush. He fled on his own airline to Brazil. Then, stricken with cancer, he returned to Switzerland for treatment. By a bizarre accident, he was recognized and arrested. He died in custody, an ailing fugitive under police arrest in Switzerland.

I remember a grim late-night vigil in a Roman villa with a king in exile who waited to know whether three of his subjects were to be summarily shot after a drumhead trial in Athens. I was there because his mother had called me. She was a friend of our family, a frequent guest in our home. Her son, she told me, needed a discreet friend with whom he could talk through the terrible dilemma that confronted him. There was no outside power he could invoke without compromising the kingship that he still held. I remember his curt but poignant farewell: "Thank you for coming. Thank you for sharing a bad evening. Now the king must make his own decision."

These are only a few of the mid-ground figures in my panorama of the years. The distant ones are more important and durable in my personal history. They must be enlarged a little because they influenced many more lives than mine and were the begetters of triumphs and tragedies they could never have dreamed of.

First, there were the Catholic clergy, grand and formal in their chesterfield coats and Roman collars and pleated stocks. These were the vanguard of an army recruited by the Congregation for the Propagation of the Faith to evangelize the young continent of Australia and the islands of the South Pacific. Many of them were Irish-born; many more were of Irish stock. They were builders of churches, schools, and hospitals. They were stout defenders of the Ancient Faith against modernism, mixed marriages, divorce, and heresy of every hue. They denied absolutely the right of error even to exist, let alone propagate itself. The sharing of prayers or rites with other churches was anathema to them. Their battle hymn was "Faith of our Fathers, living still, in spite of dungeon, fire, and sword . . ."

Among the displaced Irish and other migrant groups, they were the Lords Spiritual—temporal, too, in the end, because they held the real estate, disposed of the funds, and controlled the charities of the Church, and the votes of the people, too.

In my youth, their doughtiest champion and most Machiavellian leader was Daniel Mannix, archbishop of Melbourne, born in Ireland, onetime president of Maynooth. During the First World War, he fought and won a bitter battle against the then prime minister of Australia, a diminutive Welshman called William Morris Hughes, on the issue of conscription for military service overseas. While Ireland was in the agony of "the troubles" that followed the Easter Rebellion, Mannix planned a well-publicized visit to his homeland. The visit never took place. He was arrested off the Irish port of Queenstown and taken to England on a British destroyer—an egregious folly on the part of the British that paved the way for the partition of Ireland and self-rule for the Republic of Ireland—and in the end cost Mannix his cardinal's hat.

Both William Morris Hughes and Archbishop Mannix played important roles in my later life. After the publication of my wartime novel, *Moon in My Pocket,* Hughes appointed me as his private secretary and biographer. The reason? My publishers, who were negotiating for his autobiography, recommended me to him as "a young man of promise." He had me out of the army in three days—and fired me a few months later with a less than flattering *envoi:* "You know, West, for a moderately intelligent young man, you've done some bloody silly things. Pick up your cards and go!" I should have been abashed. I was not. I had already discovered that all his recent appointees had suffered a similar fate. The old boy taught me some tough lessons about politics that have lasted me a lifetime, and I have been dining out on his table talk and office tirades ever since!

Archbishop Mannix handed me the prize as Dux of my school in 1929. In 1951 I petitioned his marital court for a decree of nullity on my marriage. The petition was refused. I could not, would not, accept what I believed to be a loaded verdict. That verdict changed my life completely. It forced me to examine the roots and meanings of the unexamined beliefs I had held and taught for so long. It brought me to challenge publicly the canonical enactments that enforced them. It made me, for a long time, a wanderer on the face of the earth. On the other hand, it laid the foundations of my career as a novelist. It gave me the personal courage to demand an accounting from all those who claimed the right to direct my life.

After the clergy there were the educators. First in our young lives, the nuns in all their varieties of habit and vocation: the training of ladies of quality, of those who would never be ladies but might attain to respectable middle-class matronhood, of the simpler females of the servant class, and of the magdalens who, having fallen victim to the world, the flesh, and the devil could bear their children in privacy and have them adopted into good Catholic families. And if you think I am describing an old-fashioned, class-ridden, bigoted society, I am doing just that. Catholics were forbidden under pain of sin and censure to attend any kind of service in an alien church, and they prayed in the liturgy of those days for the ultimate salvation of the "perfidious Jews."

In the male order of things, which then was the dominant one—there were the Jesuits for the elite and the Brothers—Christian, Salesian, Marist, Patrician—who, supported by the funds of the faithful, undertook to drive their children out of the ghettos into open competition with the heretics of the Ascendancy: Anglicans, Presbyterians, Methodists, and the rest of the ungodly.

The Christian Brothers dominated my life for twenty-odd years. They schooled me first and then drew me—it is the most charitable word I can find—into their ranks, where I lived until the day came for me to make my vows in perpetuity, which, after a long agony of indecision, I declined to do. My servitude and its consequences are an essential element of my intellectual and spiritual life.

When I left the religious life, I was a man without a shadow. I had no past to which I could make reference, no future to which I could direct myself. In academic terms, I had a better education than most. I also carried a heavy load of unexamined certainties that I could express with the fluency of a well-trained preacher. Emotionally, I had experienced nothing but need—and for that I had no adequate vocabulary at all.

Looking back now at that distant youthful self, I see a very dangerous person—a brainwashed innocent in a world from which innocence had long absented itself, a stubborn but disciplined defender of predigested faith, and a citadel of shattered self. Worse still, I was a man stuffed so full of counsel that he could, or would, take no more. I remember the hunger for experience and the terrible ignorance of how to acquire it. Social contact was, in one sense, easy because I had been drilled to good manners and I could conduct an intelligent conversation on most subjects—no matter that, in fact, the common language that I seemed to share was an artifact unrelated to common experience. The goads that drove me were insatiable curiosity and a need, long suppressed, for a woman's companionship. On all counts, therefore, I was both vulnerable and a risk to those who came in contact with me. It took me many years to understand that I was dealing, not with a single personality as most people do, but with two selves, of which one had been suppressed so long that it had not developed at the same rate as the other. Everything I did, therefore, was marked by a kind of desperation. I was running to catch will-o'-the-wisps: lost time, lost youth, lost opportunity.

My achievements, such as they were, grew out of this desperation. I could not bear to be second-best, because in some strange way I might fade away altogether. I was unaware of the psychic burdens I carried until one magical evening when I stood within the charmed circle of the Standing Stones of Callanish in the Far Western Isles of Scotland. This is what I wrote about them:

> The place of the Standing Stones is a high grassy hump that falls away southwards towards Loch Roag with its tatter of islets and the black cliffs of Bernera heaving out of it. Even now it is a haunted spot, remote and silent always save for the crying of the gulls and the whisper of the wind through

the rank grasses. There are no trees. The hill lies naked to the sky and the great megaliths rise out of it, twice and three times the height of man. There are four avenues of them, north and south and east and west, and, at the convergence of the avenues, a circular burial place and a stone, larger than the others, which faces the sunrise. Of the men who raised the stones little is known except that they were here before the Celts— three thousand years ago—and that this hill and the surrounding countryside was a place of congress where they worshipped the sun as the source of being and plotted their ritual life by its movements. They left no language, no history. Even their burial place was despoiled before history began to be written. But they are still there, frail, tenuous ghosts.

How did I come to be there? I should have been in Africa. I had been preparing for six months to make a long tour of the whole continent—but at the last moment my courage failed me. My play *The Heretic* had taken a drubbing from the critics in London. I was tired and discouraged. My confidence was gone. I could not face a long and arduous tour alone. It was my wife who urged me out of the house, out of the family. I asked her where she expected me to go. She asked with devastating simplicity, "Why don't you go to Scotland?" Her own ancestral roots were there; mine were in another place. But her instincts were sound. She was sending me to Ultima Thule.

So, three days later I was driving westward from Inverness to God knows where. I crossed to the Isle of Skye and thence took a ferry to the tiny port of Tarbert and began driving through the uplands and peat beds of Lewis with Harris, the last island before the great Atlantic rollers. I knew no one. It was the *gaeltacht,* where the commerce of daily life is in the Gaelic, which, when you first encounter it, is a door closed in the face of the stranger, especially if he is a Sassennach.

But something strange was happening to me. I was no longer prepared to be the stranger. At night, I would pull into any farm that offered bed and breakfast, and then I would ask directions to the nearest pub, where I discovered there was usually singing and perhaps a piper or a man who played a squeeze box. I found myself singing along with the country folk, men and women. I found that I knew the words of the Gaelic songs because, long ago in my yesterdays, my masters had tried to teach me the Gaelic and some of the words had stuck, especially the words of the Island songs. So, the other man inside me began to grow taller and stronger—a fellow who could call his own tune and hold it against the counterpoint of a strange assembly. Which is not to say I was always proud of him. I came to like him, respect him, but fear him, too, because there were deep angers in him and brooding passions that sometimes came close to the boil and had either to be written out—or, more dangerously, acted out.

The Far Western Isles are rich in legends of tribal and personal conflicts. They still persist, though the stranger will hardly notice them. I even managed to write a rhyming riddle about them in the Gaelic mode:

> The man I was, the man I am
> She loves them both but surer is
> Of am than was.
> I am who am, I am who was
> I wish she'd tell the difference.

When my sojourn was over, I went back to Rome and to my family changed and, I think, cured of what ailed me. I was able to look at myself in the mirror and see my two selves and understand that I would have to live with both of them for the rest of my life, but that the living could be a harmony and not a battle. In the pub one night, the locals had christened me the

Seannachie. The *Seannach,* you see, is a bard, a storyteller, a kind of Gaelic troubadour. It's a title and an art that finally unites all the disparate parts of oneself. It expresses the gift, the grace, if you will, that holds them together, unstable though they may be. It's a title given to me by simple but subtle folk. I wear it with pride.

CHAPTER 5

SEE NAPLES *and* DIE

There is an old Italian proverb: *Chi piu sa, meno crede*— Who knows more, believes less. Read it one way, and it is a curt dismissal of superstition and credulity. Read it another, and it is a simple statement of fact: *knowing* and *believing* are mutually exclusive terms. Read it once more, and you will find yourself caught in a cobweb of questions: What is knowing; how valid is an affirmation that one knows anything? What is the nature of an act of belief? Is it an assent to a formula, or to truth itself? And that brings you at one stride to Pilate's question: "What is truth?" So, because I don't want to write and you don't want to read a long discussion on the matter, I'll tell you a story instead.

The time, March 1956, butt end of the worst European winter in a decade. The place, Naples, Italy, a ruinous, overpopulated rabbit warren of a city, with the people and the crops frost-bitten and hunger written on the pinched faces of the folk in the *bassi* and the swollen bellies of their urchin children.

Joy and I and our baby son had arrived on a vessel of the Flotta Lauro called the *Surriento,* a converted Liberty Ship that carried Italian migrants to Sydney and came back loaded with cut-price tourists like ourselves—except that we weren't tourists! We were staging a migration of our own, from a stable existence in the Australian radio industry to the gypsy life of an unproven novelist. Our assets, on arrival, were fifteen hundred dollars and a pocket full of hopes. We had decided that instead of continuing the voyage to Genoa and thence overland to London, we would spend the first spring months in the sunny, romantic south. To this end, we had cabled the Italian tourist agency C.I.T. and asked them to find us a small apartment in Sorrento.

Why Sorrento? Because I was a romantic fool with his head full of jumbled history that I was sure would somehow rearrange itself into a novel. I could speak passable Italian, but—God help me!—I had not even begun to grapple with the slurred cadences of Neapolitan and Sorrentine dialect. Worse still, I was totally unschooled in the shrugging sidelong ways of business in the Mezzogioro.

The villa we had rented was new. That much was evident. It was a concrete box cold as a tomb, the stucco still damp, the mildew already sprouting on the grouted tilework. One night in the place, and we should all be down with pneumonia. The agent was eloquently regretful. He was displeased that we were displeased. If we would be patient a little while, he would return with an electric heater. I told him he'd need a furnace day and night to heat the place. The angrier I got, the more I lost control of the language. I ended in a gibbering rage. The agent shrugged. Perhaps tomorrow he could show me an alternative residence—but it would be much, much more expensive. I asked him where the nearest hotel was. Reluctantly, he led us on foot back to an old Bourbon-style building called the Hotel Coccumella. There were renovations going on, but yes, they were open for business. They had warm rooms, and they would send a *faechino* to collect our luggage. That evening was the beginning of our long love affair with Italy.

The owner of the hotel was an American, Alison Dix Gargiulo, who had married into one of the old Bourbon families of the area. When she heard of our plight, she offered to rent us a small villa next to her own on the Via Califano. As soon as we saw the place, we fell in love with it. The ceramic tile on the portal was an omen: *Villa Gioia.* My wife's name is Joy. The rent was modest. Our landlady found us a *cameriera,* a maid of all work, a fisherman's daughter called Tina.

Tina was short, round, and durable as one of those ancient stone cannonballs. She was married, but her husband was serving a life sentence for murder. She had a daughter, Rosetta, fathered by a British soldier. Unfortunately, according to her own account, she had registered her legal husband as the father, so that when she had the chance to emigrate with relatives to Argentina, the father refused to permit the child to leave Italy. For five days a week, the little girl was cared for by the sisters in a local convent. On weekends and holidays, we had another child in the house!

That was only the first of Tina's endowments on us. The second was our own private beggar. We came upon him one morning sitting outside our iron gate, head sunk on his chest, one hand outstretched in the traditional gesture of supplication. Tina did not precisely introduce him, but she did explain him with shrugging tolerance: *"E un poveraccio, signore, vittima della guerra."* It was she who, more firmly, set the limit of his stipend. *"Cento lire, signore. Basta!"* When I suggested that a hundred lire wouldn't buy much pasta, she instructed me a little more fully. First, he would be at the gate every day except Sunday, when he worked the steps of the Cathedral of Sorrento. Second, like every self-respecting mendicant, he had his own list of daily patrons. When I asked how many that might be, she shrugged again and told me, *"Eh! N'ha parecchi"*—"He's got quite a few!" Her tone suggested that we had passed some kind of test of acceptability in the mendicant world.

Next up for adoption into our far-from-affluent household was a *cocchiere,* a coachman who drove one of the carriages that, in summer, took the tourists on scenic rides along the clifftop roads or carried them back and forth to the ferry dock on the Marina Piccola. Now we were in the middle of a brutal winter, and there were few tourists. The carriage was always brightly polished, but the coachman looked like a very under-nourished Don Quixote and his horse like Rosinante in terminal decline.

Tina explained that, as the *signora,* my wife, elected to do her own shopping, it was unseemly for her to be seen lugging bags and parcels from the market. That was servant work. She herself would be happy to do it—but then there was the question of the *bambino.* His stroller was a beautiful object, as he himself was; one did not drape it with vegetables. Joy pointed out that the village shopkeeper used a cyclist to make home deliveries. That brought us to the core of the argument: the coachman, too, was a *poveraccio.* He needed work. He was earning just enough to feed his horse. If the horse died, his livelihood would be gone.

Now I was in a dilemma. Tina, like all Italian servants, was a spendthrift with her mistress's money. My wife insisted on doing her own shopping. She liked walking into town. She didn't mind looking like a peasant. Also, at a dollar each way per day, we couldn't afford the *cocchiere.* Whatever we looked like to the townsfolk, we were living on very meager capital. I wasn't earning a nickel. In fact, I was trying to outdo the ancient alchemists and turn air into gold! However, to keep face, I consented to use the coachman *occasionally* and for a fixed price calculated per hour. It turned out to be a pyrrhic victory. Every day from then on, the coachman and his miserable beast parked outside our gate and waited and waited until one of us uttered a formal dismissal. In the south, as always, it is not the suppliant who carries the shame but the fortunate!

However, the story of the coachman was not yet over. Two evenings later I went out to the kitchen to find a second little girl digging ravenously into our biggest pasta bowl. This, Tina told me, was the coachman's daughter! What could I say? Anyone with half an eye could see the child was seriously undernourished—and she certainly didn't eat as much as a horse!

All the misfortunes of Tina's life had produced in her a fine perception of natural justice. On this question she had an ongoing *causa*—a very deep dispute—with the Almighty. She loved the religious feasts and the processions through the streets. They were beautiful, moving. They spoke to her; but Mass on Sunday—no way, not ever. Sunday was the Lord's day, yes? It was the day of *Gesu Cristo*. What had Gesu Cristo ever done for her? He had let her get married to an assassin. Because of him, she could not make a new life for her daughter. . . . Of course she was *Cattolica*, and she did go to church—on one special day of the year: the feast of San Guiseppe. Now there, Tina affirmed with absolute conviction, there was a proper man! He was the father of Gesu. He worked with his hands; he was a *falegname*, a carpenter. He knew how hard it was to put pasta on the table and warm clothes on a child's back. She talked to San Guiseppe all the time. He understood. He would try to make Gesu understand how bad things were for people like Tina.

Our landlady and her friends smiled tolerantly when I told them these small domestic comedies. I was learning, they told me. I would learn more as time went on, how rigidly and how mercilessly depressed societies structured themselves, how the haves exploited the have-nots, how the lords of the beggar kingdom—the Mafia, the Mano Nero—offered protection in return for tribute, how simple folk feared hospitals because they were places where you went to die, and how they always kept a vestige of faith in the Church, which was, at least, the gateway to a better life.

I was learning something about myself, too. To the locals I was a *forestiero*, a foreigner, but they were less foreign to me than I to them. I knew the history of their land from its earliest times. I could decipher the inscriptions in Pompeii and Herculaneum, and guess, at least, the origins of the newly excavated imperial villa on the heights above Castellamare di Stabia.

These were not things to boast about; they were discoveries about myself, long deferred fruits of a studious youth, that now, suddenly, I could recognize and enjoy. When the local folk saluted me as *Dottore,* I felt a foolish little glow of pride, a small restoration of my self-esteem, a new spurt of courage to address myself to the work that Joy had thrust at me: "There's your story! Go dig it out! There's your man, go find him!"

The man was Don Mario Borrelli, known as the Urchin Priest, who went down to live on the streets of Naples with the homeless, scavenging urchins, who shared their shabby criminal little hades, and, finally, led them, like the Pied Piper, into the shelter of an abandoned church in the back streets, the *bassi,* the low quarters of the city. I met the man. I saw what he had done. I promised to write what I could. He gave me, as guide to the underworld, one of his senior boys, who, by the way, is now a prize-winning poet and lyricist in Italy. Together we took to the streets, I in the flimsy identity of a British merchant seaman on the run from the police. This is my memory of the city we explored together in 1956:

There is a street in Naples called the Street of the Two Lepers.

To find it you must plunge into the labyrinth of lanes and alleys on the north side of the Via Roma. You must thread your way through steep, narrow ravines of houses, with lines of washing hung between them like the banners of a tatterdemalion triumph. You push through the crowds round the fruit-stalls and the fish-barrows with their mountains of mussels and trays of polypi and their tubs of slimy water crawling with snails. You brush by the hawkers with their piles of cheap cottons and second-hand jackets and patched trousers and their photographs of film stars in cheap gilt frames. You duck under the cheeses and sausages hanging from the windows of the *salumeria;* you stumble over the grubby tattered children rooting in the rubbish-piles for rinds and fruit scraps and trodden cigarette-butts. You pass a dozen shrines with dusty statues or pictures of gaudy saints behind smeared and spotted glass. The lamps glow dully and the little votive tapers flutter faintly in the chill stirring of the wind. You peer into tiny rooms where women with pinched faces bend over knitting or embroidery, or where families of ten and twelve chatter and gesticulate over bowls of steaming pasta.

Finally, you come to the Street of the Two Lepers.

There is no commerce here. It is a dark and narrow lane, whose walls are damp and slimy and whose doors are blind arches, cold and cheerless. Yet, as you pass, you see that they are astir with life. Shapeless figures sit huddled over tin dishes filled with warm charcoal ash. A bundle of rags groans and stretches out a hand in supplication. In a gloomy courtyard, where a dull lamp burns in a tiny niche, a troop of filthy children link hands and dance in a pitiful mockery of joy. The cold bites into you and you thrust your hands deeper into your pockets, duck your head under the arch of a Spanish buttress and plunge onward towards the light at the far end of the Street of the Two Lepers.

When you reach it, you find yourself in a small square with a pile of rubble in the center and a small traffic of people, gray-faced and shabby, passing and repassing from the dark lanes into the yellow light of the square and the streets of the vendors.

It was in this square that Peppino gave me my first lesson on Naples.

For me, it was an important occasion. I had dressed for it with some care. I wore an old seaman's jersey, frayed and darned in many places. My trousers were tattered and patched and I wore a pair of broken shoes with pointed toes that hurt my feet abominably. I had not shaved for three days and my nails were black and my hands were stained with grease and tobacco tar. In any other city I would have been moved on by the police, but here, in the bassi of Naples, I was dressed like a thousand others.

What I saw that night and other nights grew into a very angry book. A lot of my own private angers went into it, too. I had enough of those still to purge, but the dimension of the tragedies I had witnessed had humbled me to silence about my own.

The story of Enzo Malinconico was the story of a thousand other urchins. The tragedy of it was the tragedy of all the nameless, numberless waifs who are known as the *scugnizzi*— the spinning tops—the wild, tormented boy-children of Naples.

Enzo Malinconico was the second son of a baker who lived just north of the Via Teresa. His father was old and hard-working, his mother was young: a not uncommon combination in the Mezzogiorno, where often the old ones are the only suitors who can afford to get married. When Enzo was ten, his mother took a lover. Before he was eleven, his father found out, went crazy with jealousy, and committed suicide by burning himself in his own oven. Of his father, Enzo spoke with indifference. Whenever he mentioned his mother, he spat and called her *puttana*, which in Italy is a very dirty word indeed.

Soon after the father's suicide, the mother and her lover were married. It wasn't a very happy household. The mother was a harpy who harried both the boys and her new husband, goading them because they didn't earn enough and mocking them because they were living "on the shoulders of a woman." She herself peddled contraband cigarettes and was therefore a woman of some means!

Finally, the second husband committed suicide, and Enzo and his brother were left as the sole providers.

The brother began to sell contraband. When the police picked him up and confiscated his stock, he went to work in the market. There he established contact with a small gang who stole cases of fruit from the loading lines and sold it later around Baiae and the Porta di Capua. Finally, the police picked him up again and sent him to the grim house of correction on the little island of Procida.

Enzo was now alone with his mother. He had not yet reached his eleventh birthday.

His mother put him to work as an apprentice to a local woodworker. He swept the floor and mixed the glue and carted the timber from eight in the morning till eight at night. In the evening, his mother would fill his pockets with contraband cigarettes and send him peddling, until well after midnight.

One day Enzo ran away from home and never came back.

When the manuscript was finished, I went again to the House of the Urchins and laid it on Borrelli's desk. I told him, "There it is, Mario! It isn't enough, God knows, but it's the best I can do."

He glanced at a page or two then looked up and gave me that big, wide, streetwise grin and told me, "Mauro, at this moment, you and I are the most powerful men in the world. We have an idea. We have the words to express it—and we have nothing to lose!"

All that was forty years ago almost to the day as I pen these words. The book was published. The idea went out to the world; the work goes on to this day. I am proud of that, but I am also plagued by it in those moments of near despair that, more and more as I get older, assault my belief and my hope.

In my own city, one of the fairest and most beautiful and most prosperous in the world, there are lost children, boys and girls, prostituting themselves for survival. There are feral and evil folk who exploit them without mercy. The scandal is public and shameful, but it still goes on. The young ones are already in despair. We, the old ones, are damned by our own surrender to the subtlest evil of all, indifference! We make effigies of goodness. We dress them up in copes and miters and cassocks. We create elaborate rituals of respect for them. We create effigies of evil, too, stock figures of gangsters and assassins and larcenous villains. But, in fact, the true face of good is often smudged and weary and battle-scarred, while the face of evil is plump and smiling, bland and golden as honey.

CHAPTER 6

A PERCEPTION *of* EVIL

What I have to tell you now was triggered by a series of totally unrelated events.

A dear friend of ours called to tell us that her daughter, a woman of forty, had been followed to her house, brutally beaten, and repeatedly raped by an unknown assailant.

Custodians of infant children in a fashionable day-care center near my home were arrested for sexual abuse of their tiny charges.

Three teenagers and two young adults kidnapped, raped, and murdered a young businesswoman returning home after a day's work.

There was a report of a new clinic set up to rehabilitate the victims of professional torture, which is taught and practiced in the armed services and the intelligence cadres of so-called civilized countries—my own among them.

Every day the headlines screamed new revelations of violence, of bribery, corruption, and criminal affiliations among our police and politicians.

Even the financial pages were full of the plots and counterplots, the sieges and betrayals of our business leaders, who were fighting like robber barons for new fiefdoms.

There was something obscene in the spectacle of their naked greed. There was something terrifying in the breakdown of the fiduciary relationship between the people and their elected representatives, the people and the public servants whom they paid to protect their fundamental rights. There was stark horror in the total amorality of criminal children, and a worse one still in those who pimped and pandered them in our city streets.

The more I thought about these things, the more I became haunted by the naked reality, the dark, repetitive mystery of evil in the world. We had learned nothing from the Holocaust, from the genocide in Kampuchea, the long bloody agonies of war in the Middle East.

Why is it so? Why do we rational creatures act so perversely, so destructively? What begets this monstrosity? What keeps it alive and reproducing itself?

These are no new questions. They are woven into the most ancient cosmologies, the most diverse philosophies. For the Greeks, the origin of evil was in matter itself. For the Gnostics and Manichaeans, evil was present from the beginning, a malignant principle rooted in matter and darkness, waging eternal war with a principle of good rooted in the spirit and in light.

Either notion raises an even greater ugliness in the human mind: that the source of evil is the Creator Himself—that what we call God is a cruel absurdist, presiding over a chaos of His own making. Plotinus, greatest of the Neoplatonist philosophers, proposed an answer to the terrifying riddle. Evil, he said, was not a principle, nor was it self-existent. It was simply the absence of good, a collapse of light into solid blackness, like the dark holes in the galaxies.

But, profound as the idea was and still remains, it cannot cushion the shock of the *experience* of evil by the human person, the sheer, inescapable, destructive, totally indifferent power of it. This is the real terror of modern torture. It is designed by intelligent beings to achieve the total degradation of a human person, the annihilation of dignity and will, by an exercise of cruelty based upon supreme indifference and illusory omnipotence.

In like manner, the invasion of one's person or one's family by criminal violence—rape, violent assault, murder—creates a trauma so profound that the scars may never disappear. The notion of irreversible evil has driven many to suicide.

So, in the faith of Israel there appeared another concept of evil, one less tolerable, more fruitful in hope than the speculations of philosophers. It was the concept of sin, a deliberate and knowing breach of the relationship between creature and Creator. From this breach, called original or primal sin, all evil issued, like the plagues from Pandora's box. The sin was prompted by a tempter, the serpent, the Evil One, but committed by primal man and primal woman, free agents made in the likeness of their Creator.

Punishment followed. Paradise was lost. Mankind was exiled into a hostile wilderness from which it could be rescued only by penitence on the part of the creature, by the grace and favor of a redemptive act by the Creator. The way to the lost paradise was opened again, but it was a road haunted and beset always by the adversary, the Evil One, Satan, with his legions of damned spirits who had chosen rather to reign in hell than serve in heaven.

But, even in the biblical narratives, the old dualist notion reasserted itself; evil was again personified in the Demon. The origin and nature of evil were described in other metaphors, but it remained, as it remains still, an unsolved mystery.

I hold my infant grandchild in my arms, and I experience a wonderful, tender joy at the physical perfection and the fragile, dependent innocence of this tiny creature. Yet I know that the genetic imprints she has inherited from me and from others will determine her health or her illness in later life. I see her now, surrounded and supported by love on all sides, yet I know that a day will come when she will step outside the charmed circle and assert her right to be a free woman and make her own choices about her own destiny.

She will be vulnerable then to the random malice of the world, to her own passions, to all the wonderful, perilous illusions of youth. She, like all of us, will be tempted to despair when those illusions shatter under the impact of cruel reality.

I can spare her none of this. I cannot even prepare her for it. Evil, you see, is not explainable. It is not even understandable. It is what the writers of the *Dutch Catechism* called "the great absurdity, the great irrelevancy."

It is absurd in the sense that disease is absurd—a tumor in the brain can turn a genius into a vegetable; a chemical imbalance can turn the gentlest of creatures into a raving maniac. It is irrelevant in the sense that, like the Black Death in the Middle Ages or AIDS in our time, it conforms to no logic that we can grasp or rely upon.

Yet the metaphor is apt. Evil is contagious. Like the anthrax bacillus in the soil, it lies dormant in all of us, but when it breaks out of its capsule, it becomes a wildfire infection. Violence begets violence. Daily exposure to cruelty or pornography desensitizes the human person to the pain of others, to guilt, to the grossest indecencies.

Seduce or brutalize a child, and you create a casualty or a criminal. Bribe a servant of the state, and you will soon hear the deathwatch beetles chewing away at the rooftrees of society. The disease of evil is pandemic; it spares no individual, no society, because all are predisposed to it.

It is this predisposition that is the root of the mystery. I cannot blame a Satan, a Lucifer, a Mephistopheles, for the evils I have committed, the consequences of which have infected other people's lives. I know, as certainly as I know anything, that the roots are in myself, buried, deeper than I care to delve, in caverns so dark that I fear to explore them. I know that, given the circumstances and the provocation, I could commit any crime in the calendar.

The fact that I have not run through them all is due in part to what an elderly uncle of mine would have called "circumstantial salvation," which he explained by saying that the reason he had never committed adultery was that he had been lucky enough never to meet a woman who pleased him more than his wife!

But just as I am conscious of a capacity for evil in myself, I am equally conscious of its opposite: a capacity for good and an ability to distinguish it. I aspire to it, though I do not always attain it. I recognize that the attainment is often beyond my strength unless I am supported and aided by others. So, even in purely natural terms, I find myself open to the Christian concept of *grace:* the gift, the aid that enables me to accomplish that which is beyond my single strength.

I am equally open to the belief in divine forgiveness as an absolute necessity in the pursuit of good. I am the father of a family, the patriarch of an extending one. I know that the family cannot hold together—more, that it will utterly destroy itself—unless its members learn to forgive one another their small and their large delinquencies. They have to learn, too, from their earliest years to forgive themselves as a necessary prelude to forgiving others. They have to be taught to perceive in the mirror the God-image behind the often distorted and self-hating human one.

I believe in free will. I believe that I am capable of making a choice between good and evil. I know, however, that neither I nor anyone else is wholly free. Our liberty is abridged in a thousand ways: by physical and psychic dispositions, by ignorance, by fear, by economic pressure, by lack or simple overload of information. So our perception of evil as absolute must never cloud our perception of guilt as a relative matter.

Murder is a deed most foul and most final. I stand firm in that conviction. Face me with the murderer, I may wish to slay him with my own hands, but I must, on the contrary, protect him until he is brought to fair judgment by his peers. If I abdicate this standing ground, then I open the way to vendetta, a death for every death, down the generations. There are many in our society who advocate solutions almost as draconian. A crime, they say, is an irreversible act. The contagion of the evil continues to spread. The punishment must be condign and merciless, a permanent deterrent. On the other hand, they commit themselves to a more dangerous proposition, that the criminal himself is an irreversible being.

No one will deny that there are some such—individuals so molded, set, and fixed into a pattern of evil that there is no human hope of change. To these, the old formulary of the hanging judge seems to apply: ". . . and may God have mercy on your soul." But what of the others, the still reformable, the genuine casualties of a society that has too little care or compassion for its own children and watches them thrown on the trash heap without a tremor of compunction? Should we not ask ourselves whether we are not the evildoers and they the ultimate victims because we have denied them their true birthright: the experience of love and a parental instruction in the difference between good and evil?

But I have not yet addressed myself to the question that triggered all these reflections. Is there a Devil, a Dark Angel, a Satan, a true spiritual Prince of Darkness, who, to use the biblical phrase, "goeth about like a roaring lion seeking whom he may devour"?

Let me be open and say that he would be a bold scribe indeed who would gainsay the existence of a figure who looms so large and so majestic in biblical utterance and in the mythologies of Europe. All the Christian churches have ceremonies of exorcism for the driving out of evil spirits, and the most ancient sacramental rite of baptism, by which one enters the Christian assembly, contains a specific renunciation of "Satan and all his works."

However, be he symbol or personage, the image of Satan is potent and malefic. He represents the whole gamut of evil and its power to perpetuate itself as an infection in the human race. On the other hand, let it never be forgotten that it was belief in Satan as a personage, and a barbaric view of his presence and powers in human affairs, that led to the vilest excesses of Christendom, the witch-hunts of the twelfth to the sixteenth centuries. A single quote will suffice to make the point: "Men and women straying from the Catholic faith have abandoned themselves to *incubi* and *succubi* [male and female sexual partners] and by their incantations, spells, conjurations and other accursed offenses, have slain infants yet in their mother's womb, as also the offspring of cattle" (Bull of Pope Innocent VIII, *Summis desiderantes affectibus,* December 1484).

That document was the beginning of inquisitions and massacres that went on in the Old World for nearly three centuries and were contained in the New in the witch trials of Salem.

With all the evil that we are able to devise for ourselves, a personal Prince of Darkness seems a redundancy! More, it raises the much more vexing question of the eternity and immortality of evil—which to me is a notion utterly contradictory to the "restoration of all things in Christ." Much closer to our own epoch and experience, perhaps, is the expression *Powers of Darkness.*

The plural word expresses aggregation, collective action, collective strength. It is precisely thus that we have seen the most monstrous evils of our time brought to pass: Europe tyrannized and tumbled to ruins by collectivist philosophies—Fascism, Nazism, Stalinism; the Holocaust committed in a

collective conspiracy of silence; the South American dictator-
ships buttressed by U.S. presidential policies; the drug barons creating their new empires with the new currency of
narcotics—so much more stable than paper and gold, so much
more valuable than human lives; the Middle East turned into a
battleground over oil and God.

Darkness may seem an inapposite word for an epoch in
which global communication is instantaneous and continuous. But sinister things are happening. More and more of the
organs of communication are falling into fewer and fewer
hands. The battle for the audience dollar to finance the net-
works is becoming so intense that the talents of the commu-
nicators are being suborned to serve the lowest common
denominator of the audience. The power to impose a darkness of the intellect and call it light is now an immediate fact.
Because it exists, it can and will be used. Maybe we simple
folk will have to do as the old Romans did—keep a gaggle of
geese to warn us of the invaders.

In the face of such collective power, such an assembly of illusory wisdom, we individuals often seem ludicrously impotent.
Confused, conscious of our own many shortcomings, we are
easily tempted into silence and submission by the big battal-
ions. The small capital of good that we possess, that we hug to
our bosoms like the last talisman of an old faith, seems pitifully
inadequate against the new brazen gods whose images adorn
the triumphal way.

Nevertheless, this is how the battle of good against evil always begins: one small voice raised in the crowd, proclaiming
that the king has no clothes, that the new gods are hollow plaster, that the new masters in the land are crooks and charlatans.
Until that voice is raised, the tyranny will continue. Once it is
heard, courage, like crime, proves contagious, and the tattered
banners are raised once more against the ancient adversary.

Yet, sometimes words fail us, because good folk are much less certain of themselves than evil ones. The very fact that we reach out for truth and goodness, search for them painfully and patiently, implies that we do not yet possess them in fullness and certainty or that, possessing them, we do not yet recognize their full worth.

Do I seem to exaggerate? Let me tell you a true story from my Roman days. One of our neighbors was an elderly German lady with a name well known in modern history and long financial connections in Brazil and Argentina. She was ill and needed company in her black moments. We visited occasionally. On one of these visits I met one of her sons, a wealthy industrialist. We talked about the Squadrons of Death, the vigilante killers then operating in Brazil, murdering dissidents and protesters. He assured me quite blandly, not only that he considered them a social necessity, but that he and his business colleagues financed their activities.

I gaped at him in silence, wondering why I felt no anger, no impulse to violence, only a sick, sad disgust. Then we took our leave of his mother and went home. It was at that moment, I think, I learned the hardest lesson of my life. Evil is serene in its enormity. Evil is indifferent to argument or to compassion. It is not merely the absence of good; it is the absence of everything human, the black hole in a collapsed cosmos in which even the face of God is eternally invisible.

From this ultimate damnation there is no recourse. No light can penetrate the dense core of tangible darkness. *Enfer c'est le néant*—Hell is nothingness. For the rest of us, there remains still the pilgrimage, the journey in hope and mutual caring toward the ultimate revelation of eternal Goodness. It is not for nothing that the symbols of that hope are a star still blazing in the heavens and a babe, newborn, sleeping in a manger with dumb and innocent animals for guardians.

CHAPTER 7

THE RESPONSE
to VIOLENCE

I remember as if it were yesterday—though it is now eighteen years past—the night I wrote the last words of *Proteus*. It was ten minutes after midnight. My eyes were burning. My bloodstream was full of caffeine. My pulse was racing, and some old Egyptian was drilling holes in my skull.

I switched off the lights, flung open the window, and stood a long time staring out at the ghostly garden. The lawns and the flower beds lay placid under the full moon. The woodland fringe heaved up, black against the sky. I heard the hooting of the owl that lived in the big walnut tree. Far down in the hollow a vixen screamed. I felt suddenly empty, and alone. I was sixty-two years old, and I was very, very afraid.

The vixen screamed again—a haunting, feral sound. I imagined her mating in the dark forest. I remembered—how strange the tricks of memory!—the Place of the Standing Stones in the far Hebrides, where once I had come face to face with my *döppelganger* and been terrified of him because he looked like a red wolf.

I should have been elated. My book was done. Three long years of servitude were over. There was time now to eat, drink, and be merry. I had spent sweat, love, and anger; but I had done craftsman's work and I had no reason to be ashamed of it.

I have a habit that makes my family smile. I pat a finished manuscript. I fondle it and dandle it as a woman plays with a child. But this time was different. The pages lay untouched on my desk. I was afraid of them—because of what I had written, because of what the pages might do once they passed out of my control and were absorbed into the brains of other men and women. I was like an armorer, proud of the sword blade he had fashioned but suddenly aware of blood upon the damascene.

Before the manuscript passed out of my hands, I had to make an accounting with myself, because, like it or not, I was accountable to others and, in the end, to whatever God gave me being.

The vixen was silent now, mated and assuaged. The owl in the walnut tree was dumb. In the house across the lawn my family slept. Who was I? Why was I? What strange, ironic destiny had led me to this cold moment, in a silent place, a moment in which it seemed I held the key to Pandora's box. If I opened the box, what would fly out? Only new terrors? Or perhaps a small, bright hope?

I was deathly tired but drugged with black coffee. I knew I could not sleep. My mind was spinning like a mill saw that, at any moment, might explode into lethal fragments. Had there been anyone to listen, I could have talked the night away, but there was no one. I remembered the sweet, childish tale my beloved aunt told me: that God made Adam because He was lonely in His splendid universe and needed someone to talk to.

"Proteus" was a god, too, albeit a minor one. Poseidon appointed him shepherd of all the sea creatures, endowed him with all knowledge, and, for protection of his secrets, gave him the power to change himself at will into a multitude of shapes: a bird, a flower, a lion, a flame of fire. To the ancient Orphics he became a symbol of primal magma, origin of all being, all the good and evil in the world. I had used his name as the title of my book because I was writing about the conflict of good and evil in this, the age of assassins.

The evil for me was specific: the violence practiced upon man by his fellows—the invasion of the human person by professional torturers, interrogators, jailers, paid assassins, kidnappers, medical men who debased the art of healing. The question that I posed in fiction—because people accept a truth in fiction that they refuse to face in fact—was simple enough.

What will be your response, what will be mine, when violence touches us and our loved ones? Yet, when I came to write, I found that the simple question had turned into a riddle more complex and terrifying than I had expected. "If I act, I become one of them. If I act not, I become their slave." And the first answer to the riddle—perhaps the last one possible—was, "God give me light."

The only light left to me on that solitary night was the lume of a dead planet, full of the bane of old enchantments. I had, like the philosopher in my novel, written myself into a corner. There was no way out of it except by a leap of faith, which truly, at that moment, was impossible to me. I was forced to conclude—however reluctantly—that man is a mad animal, dedicated, by an almost universal death wish, to his own destruction.

I am, normally, an optimistic man. I have learned to count blessings, to be grateful for winter sun and the sudden smile. However, the country that I had inhabited those last three years—the domain of high politics and high business—is a sinister one. Its language is wry on the tongue, inept for poetry or the making of songs. There are no philosophers in its think tanks, no troubadours beneath its barred windows. Its folk wear cynicism like a sidearm in the streets, and, when they meet in Parliament or on the Bourse, they leave their hearts at home.

I had learned much from them: how costly it is to insure a bank president against kidnapping for ransom, how cheap it is to hire a professional killer, how ministers of state are blackmailed and public servants suborned. I had studied the new black arts: how to torture a woman with an electric current, induce madness by sensory deprivation, debase the most noble intellect with psychotropic drugs—and how to justify it all by a well-turned editorial or an impassioned speech in the Assembly.

To learn so much, I had practiced a sedulous urbanity. I could sit, smiling, while my host proclaimed his hatred of "niggers on television" and the salutary effect of napalm, land mines, and defoliants. I could nod sagely as the Latin American diplomat explained that order and progress had often to be paid for in blood, and that fear kept the garden more safely than the gardener. I had been silent so long. I found that silence had begun to corrupt me. I had reasoned so much with unreason that I had begun to suspect my own indignation. I was like a victim of the old inquisitors, so confused by questioning, so seduced by subtleties, that he would sign anything, surrender everything, for the simple mercy of sleep.

The owl hooted again. Far away through the trees, I saw the lights of the police car that patrolled our estate to keep us privileged ones free from marauders. The patrol would stop by my cottage. Seeing my light, a young policeman would knock and inquire respectfully if all was well. I would be grateful for his care. And I would remember with a pang of guilt this colleague and that, languishing in prison cells, cut off from all human concern, because they had said once, and bluntly, what I had taken three years to debate in private before I wrote.

I closed the window, sat down at my desk, and drank the last bitter cup of cold coffee. I picked up the manuscript and weighed it in my hands—weighing myself with it. Enough of argument! Enough of silence! What I had written, I had writ-

ten. Let it go! Let other men judge the document, while I made reckoning with my own self.

I remembered a day, eighteen years ago, when I collapsed by a swimming pool in California. It was a moment of bitter irony. I was newly known, newly prosperous. *The Devil's Advocate* was on the best-seller list; it was running as a play on Broadway. *Daughter of Silence* was ready for launching. I was halfway through the stage version. Lucrative commissions were being offered to me every week. Suddenly, without warning, I was in hospital with a massive pulmonary invasion that seemed to defy diagnosis. I was tested for a whole gamut of diseases: TB, Q fever, psittacosis—all negative. I seemed to be getting better, then I relapsed twice. Came the day when my doctor announced that he would like to do a biopsy. I asked why. He told me that there remained only two possible diagnoses. Either I was suffering from an atypical virus infection or a lymphatic cancer. A biopsy would provide conclusive evidence. Without the biopsy? Either I would get better in a couple of weeks, or I would be under sentence of death. I resented the thought of yet another invasion of my ravaged person. I said I would like to think about it. The doctor nodded, patted my hand, and left me. I burst into tears.

By the time evening came, I had recovered sufficiently to be rational with my family, but when they had gone, I lay sweating in a solitude so bleak that I thought I should go crazy. A small painless operation, a simple pathological test, would tell me the truth within a day. I was not ready to face it. Rather than accept a summary death sentence, I would prefer to sweat out two weeks of terror and two weeks of hope, however tenuous and illusory.

I remembered the opening sentence of *The Devil's Advocate*, which the critics—remote and unimportant now!—had called a masterwork: "It was his profession to prepare other men for death; it shocked him to be so unready for his own." It was the first of many things I have written that, without my knowing, had a touch of prophecy in them.

The next evening, I told the doctor I would prefer to wait out the time without a biopsy. He discharged me, still unrecovered, and let me go home. The outcome was fortunate. I am still alive, but the memory of that siege and the emotions I experienced has hung over everything I have since done and written.

I learned in the war the value and the fragility of human life. I learned to loathe those who disprized it, who treated men and women like beasts, debasing them by intimidation and calculated cruelty. I am older now. I have come to terms with dying, but with cruelty and debasement—never!

Herein lies the reason for my near despair during the writing of *Proteus*. The lessons of the war had been forgotten. The nightmares of Auschwitz and the ultimate horror of Hiroshima were a dim memory. Even in the most tolerant and civilized society, cruelty was and still is used as an official instrument of social control.

The cruelty takes many forms: harassment of dissidents and their families, restriction of movement, censorship, house arrest, preventive detention, forcible segregation, sensory deprivation, the use of mind-changing drugs, starvation, and the most barbaric physical tortures. No country is guiltless in this matter.

American experts had taught the black art to their colleagues in Latin America, Vietnam, Iran, and Korea. The Marxist states were old practitioners of the discipline of fear. Most sinister of all, the public had been conditioned for a long time to a new mythos of violence. Many a time, I had been tempted to believe that the conditioning was too deep to be reversed.

Recently, I read with wry amusement a news item about a priest who volunteered to take a lie-detector test on television.

During the interrogation he was asked, "Do you believe in God?" He answered, "I do." The detector recorded his answer as a lie! I chuckled at his embarrassment, but I pitied him too. Life itself is the best of all lie-detectors. All of us carry around with us a baggage of unexamined credos and untested convictions. All of us discover, soon or late, what cobwebs we have clung to in the dark.

The man with the license to kill is a cult figure in fiction and in fact. It is time, I believe, to stop and force the questions: Licensed by whom? Under whose law? With what possible justification? Unless the syndrome can be broken, there will be no end to the bloody cycle of terror and counterterror, of anarchy and state repression. But how to break it in a free society?

The dictators and oligarchs claim that their answer is the only one that will work: total censorship to stifle dangerous thoughts, total repression so that dissidents cannot organize and act. It is the oldest solution in the book: crush the infamous thing, wipe out the false prophets and their followers, and then we shall have peace in the land. In our so-called free society we affect to deny the insidious proposition, but at every level of government we mimic the tyrants. Intimidation is used, along with blackmail and unauthorized surveillance and unconstitutional secrecy, to silence critics and discourage inquiry.

It is, of course, the logic of insanity. Censorship discredits the censor. Tactics of terror set the state in perpetual vendetta with its own citizens. The underground press flourishes. Religious leaders mount repressive action against dissidents. Partisans make bombs in their kitchens. Open any newspaper, switch on your television, and the symptoms of the sickness are manifest: a bomb blast in Jerusalem, a genocide in Rwanda, a massacre in Sri Lanka.

I travel much. Every time I enter an airport, there are armed guards and body searches by security men. I am supposed to be grateful for their protection. I feel rather that I am trapped in a repetitious nightmare of menaces and mayhem.

And yet I am one of the privileged—born in a free country, endowed with enough talent to earn a good living in my profession. So far, thank God, the violence has not touched me or my family. But what if it did? What if it were my son battered to death in a police cell, my daughter violated by the interrogators of a secret police?

At a moment of crisis men and women look instinctively for pragmatic solutions: the power play of diplomacy and economic pressure. When these fail, the next inevitable recourse is vendetta: the violent response to the violent act. The moment this step is taken, the rest of the scenario is inevitable. One death determines another, and the violence escalates in an exponential curve to the dimensions of a global threat. The mushroom in the cow pasture suddenly becomes a mushroom cloud, infecting everything within the perimeter of its fallout.

Men and women of absolute faith and absolute integrity are rare on our shabby planet. When I was in Rome for the obsequies of Pope John Paul I, I heard gossip that he might have been, could have been, poisoned. Later, a book was written claiming that the gossip was truth. I dismissed the book publicly because I believed it was a defective bill of particulars and an unsound conclusion. What I could not dismiss was the readiness of even religious folk to entertain malice, to justify it by historic precedent. So much of our human commerce is based upon the cynical presumption of probable guilt. The bloody sheet must be displayed to prove the bride was virgin. Contracts are drawn to provide sanctions against default. Oaths are administered, because without them—and often with—men will give false testimony. No dedication is selfless. No motive is wholly pure.

It is precisely in this cynicism that the seeds of our madness flourish. Reject all idea of grace—of soul-gifts transcending our imperfection—reject all aspiration to a spiritual betterment, and what is left? Only a single proposition: Man is a malicious animal who must be tamed. If he will not respond to gentling, then beat him. If, still, he will not submit, then kill him, for a caution to the rest.

For me, it is a base and brutal philosophy. Yet I am constantly shocked by the many who find it acceptable. One can sometimes forgive the politicians who are corrupted into insensibility by the sheer mass of the problems that confront them, but the private men, the private women, who are dedicated to the disciplines of fear haunt me like the ghosts of the Belsen jailers.

I had a friend, now dead, who had been very kind to me. He fought in the Pacific War. He spent half a lifetime as a trader in Southeast Asia. During the Tet offensive, he was taken prisoner by the Vietcong and spent nearly a year in a hole in the ground in various jungle camps. Yet, when I talked to him about the monstrous events in Cambodia—the slaughter of thousands, the total evacuation of the cities, the brutal collectivization of the populace—he shrugged and smiled and said, "Maybe they're right. Maybe this is the only way to do it." "To do what?" I asked. "Organize the bloody place. Get it working like a modern state with a chance in the twentieth century. Once they're getting the best out of their resources, they can always breed back the people they've killed."

After that, what could I say? There was no ground of argument. We might have been men from different planets, our talk a Babel-chatter signifying nothing.

I remember other, similar dialogues of the mad: with the diplomat in Vietnam who saw the impending assassination of

President Diem as the only sure way to peace, with the aging cardinal in Rome who still justified the Inquisition because error had no right to exist and man's only fundamental right was to acknowledge the truth and live by it, with the Australian prime minister who thought that a "small war" in Asia would be a good proving ground for our Australian troops.

Do I believe in God? Yes, I do, though I cannot reason Him into existence, though I do not believe all that is written, or approve all that is done, in His name. I believe that all creation is a mask of God, and the most diverse creeds cloak an essential truth.

What do I believe about man? That he is a perverse animal, prone sometimes to insanity. That he is improvable but never, never perfectible. That brutality will debase him, and that only love and respect and forgiveness can ennoble him.

I have written here a harsh truth, because life is harsh and dangerous and there are no easy answers to its dilemmas. God is not everywhere, or always in evidence in his own creation. But I have not written without love or without hope. I have simply tried to show what human life may be when love and hope are absent. It will be winter then, the beginning of the new Ice Age. I fear for my children who may have to endure it. For my part, I would rather not be here to see it.

CHAPTER 8

THE HERETIC *and the* DIGNITY *of* DISSENT

O n the seventeenth day of February in the year of our Lord 1600, a man called Giordano Bruno was burned for heresy in that place which is called the Field of Flowers in Rome.

On the ninth day of June 1889 on the same spot, representatives of the faculty and students of the University of Rome unveiled a statue of Bruno executed by the sculptor Ettore Ferrari. A medal was struck to commemorate the event. The inscription on the medal reads:

> To Giordano Bruno—
> The Century he guessed at—
> In Rome,
> Where he was burned at the stake.

I lived for seven years in Rome from the mid-sixties to 1972. I had walked a hundred times past the great, hooded, brooding figure in the Campo dei Fiori. I had seen it lit by the flames of the bonfires when the market folk burned their refuse in the square at the end of a winter's day. Always on those occasions I had felt myself oppressed by the same enormous weight that crushed him, the weight of power, of the vast interest invested in orthodoxy, be it political, religious, or scientific.

Finally, I set myself to search out Bruno's work, to collate the fragmentary records of his trials in Venice and Rome, to reconstruct his portrait from the scribbles on the palimpsest of history. I found him, like all of us, a contradictory character: a muddled philosopher, an arrogant scholar, a boaster in his cups, a poet in his quiet hours, scared, venal, compromising— and yet, in sum, a figure of heroic proportions.

He was born in Nola, in the south of Italy. At an early age he joined the Order of Friars Preachers. Later, he fled the monastery and became a wandering scholar. He taught and wrote all over Europe. He was lector to the king of France. He disputed at Oxford and Wittenberg. He spent a brief time in the entourage of Sir Phillip Sydney at the court of Elizabeth I. There is evidence that he acted as a spy for Sir Francis Walsingham, principal secretary to Queen Elizabeth I, who wanted England to join herself with Protestant and Catholic powers in Europe. It was Walsingham who contrived the famous Babington conspiracy, which led to the execution of Mary, Queen of Scots.

Like so many scholars before and after him, Bruno was tempted into the dangerous games of power. His ambition outran his influence, and he was forced to leave England and try to restore his flagging fortunes in Europe. Finally, in 1592 he came to Venice. Giovanni Mocenigo, scion of a dogal family, engaged him as a tutor in magical arts, to assist him to regain the doge's cap that his uncle, Alvise, had lost when he lost Cyprus to the Turks. When no magic was forthcoming, Mocenigo denounced him to the Inquisition as a heretic. Imprisoned, interrogated, and tortured in Venice, he recanted. Then the Romans claimed him. After seven more years of confinement and inquisition, he refused a second recantation that might have saved his life and given him back his liberty.

The better I knew him, the more modern I found him, the more relevant to our epoch in which knowledge explodes but mysteriously deepens every day. We think we are freer than he, whereas in reality we are bound more stringently. Burning is no longer a fashionable penalty, but the torturers are still on the public payroll, the death squads are out, somewhere, every night.

You see, it is the illusion of our time that the nonconformist is in the ascendant, that the heretic is the hero and the revolutionary is the new redeemer.

In fact, the odd man out has never been so much at risk or so competently menaced by that conspiracy of power that we are pleased to call government. The mechanics of social control are more sophisticated than they have ever been in history, most sophisticated in those countries where the legal and judicial odds seem loaded in favor of the individual.

The extremist position—left or right—is at least clear: deviate and you are damned—to expulsion from the Party, to bread-line subsistence, to a limbo of nonpersons, to a brutal confinement, to death without honor. The democratic method is more subtle but hardly less effective. The taxing authority may invade your most private transactions, and what it cannot prove it may presume in default of contrary evidence. An employer may solicit, file, and transmit, without your consent, the most intimate details of your private life—and your refusal to communicate them may provide a presumption of hidden delinquencies.

The social spy, the wire tapper, and the peddler of devices to violate privacy have become stock personages in our society; the growth of large monopolies in communication has forced the protester into the streets and the parks, where protest may easily be construed or manipulated into a public disorder. A whole industry has been built around the art of affirmation, but the dignity of dissent is daily denigrated. The doubter is in disgrace because he or she demands time to reflect before committing to an act of faith. The liberty most laborious to maintain is the liberty to be mistaken.

But the threat to the odd one out is not merely external. It is internal as well. So much diverse information, so many divergent opinions are poured into our eyes and ears that the effort to rationalize them all threatens, at times, our very sanity. Often our only salvation is to call a halt, to say, "I do not know. I cannot commit until I do know. I will not commit without the time and freedom that you refuse to grant me." I myself have been caught in this syncope. I myself have been subject to the most artful and powerful pressures to force me to proclaim that which others believe to be true but which I cannot in good conscience profess.

After the breakdown of my first marriage, I applied to the diocesan court of the Holy Roman Rota for a decree of annulment as a prelude to civil proceedings for divorce. My plea was rejected. I presented myself at the archbishop's office for an explanation. His vicar-general offered me a new problem to cap the old one. I remember the text of it almost verbatim.

"The evidence in support of your plea was insufficient. We agree that, in the internal form of conscience you may, in fact, not be married. However, in default of further evidence in the external forum, we must conclude that the bond is still valid."

What I was hearing, of course, was the old rule *favor matrimonii*. In other words, the institution of marriage must be favored and not the persons involved in it.

My reply was blunt. The verdict was unjust. The law itself was unjust. I would accept neither. The vicar-general expressed regret and compassion. He told me I could appeal to Rome. I told him I had no money to do that. What was I expected to do with the rest of my life? He then advised me that if I married again outside the Church, it would mean automatic excommunication. I told him that was an added injustice. He affirmed reluctantly that, according to the canons, I might live discreetly in concubinage without incurring the penalty of excommunication. I told him that if they wanted me out of the Church, they should arrange it formally and openly. Unless they were prepared to do that, I should be seen and known everywhere as a professing Catholic, denied the justice of the assembly. The vicar-general shrugged unhappily, and I took my leave—a very angry man.

What followed was a separation and then a divorce. I remarried in a civil ceremony. We have four children, who were all baptized and educated in the Catholic faith. My own battle for reform and for simple justice continued.

So it came to pass that, nearly thirty years later, I sat in my Roman garden correcting the proofs of a book called *Scandal in the Assembly,* which my co-author and I had subtitled *A Bill of Complaints and a Proposal for Reform on the Matrimonial Laws and Tribunals of the Roman Catholic Church.* The publication took place five years after the end of the Second Vatican Council, three years after the encyclical *Sacendotalis Celibatus* on priestly celibacy, and two years after the fateful publication of *Humanae Vitae,* the papal ruling against artificial methods of birth control.

I had studied much and learned much—suffered, too— during the intervening years. I had been established for more than five years as a resident in Rome. I had served briefly as a special correspondent at the Vatican for the *Daily Mail* of London. The list of my published works included *Children of the Sun, The Devil's Advocate,* and *The Shoes of the Fisherman.* All these books were centered upon the Church and the communion of faith within its visible and invisible body. I was, as I had sworn I would be, a very visible and very vocal member of the Christian assembly.

A new code of canon law was still being drafted. My conversations with bishops and canonical theologians during Vatican II had given me hope of a solution. But my hopes, like those of many others, were fading rapidly under the unsteady hand of Pope Paul VI, and I had determined to publish an open appeal for an accurate restatement of the Christian theology of marriage and a restoration of the compassionate intent of the most ancient traditions of the Church. My thesis was, and is, in the direct line of that tradition:

> In the Roman Catholic Church, as it is constituted today, the communicating member or the non-communicant who falls under its laws has no legal recourse against the law or the lawmaker. He, or she, is subject to statutes that exist, good or bad. No procedure exists by which men and women can challenge their validity or even their doctrinal foundations. They recognise a principle of authority, but they cannot protect themselves against its unlawful or injudicious exercise.
>
> We accept the prescription of law that, once canonical requirements are fulfilled, a Christian marriage exists; but we accept it as a presumption and not as a proven fact. If the marriage breaks down irretrievably, there is another presumption, equally reasonable, that the parties lacked the capacity to achieve a Christian union in the sacramental sense of the word. Therefore, a reasonable doubt exists as to the validity of the union. Therefore, the persons must be favoured and not the institution. Marriage was made for men and women. The Church must not chop and lop them to make them fit it, as if the marital couch were a bed of Procrustes.

If you ask me why, after all these years and some real reforms in the canons and in practice, I make so much of this personal issue, I will answer you plainly. This was the struggle that determined what I am today: a believer by choice. I am not, I can never be, a complaisant one. There were many times when it would have been easier for me to quit the Church than to support the injustice she imposed, not only on me but on many others, good and brave men and women, who cherish "the liberty of the Spirit in the bond of faith." For good or ill, I elected to stay and exercise my right to speak openly as an advocate for justice and mercy in the assembly of the faithful.

Time, and the providential ordering that it brings, has healed old wounds. I, too, have learned something of the art of healing and have tried to pass it on, like old Hippocrates to his pupils. It says something, I suppose, for the uses of adversity that the bewildered young man who walked out of the convent gates fifty-six years ago is still on his feet and still able to record with equanimity those long-ago battles. It leads me to another, more agreeable confession: the debt I owe my present wife, the mother of my second family. It is she who has taught me tolerance and calmed my combative spirit and provided the haven within which I have been able to contemplate the human comedy and to discern some small part of the divine drama.

It was she who showed me that the key to forgiving and to being forgiven is love. She also taught me the hardest lesson of all, that we have to forgive ourselves before we are ready to ask forgiveness of God or man. None of us can survive a vendetta with the person we see every day in the mirror. We have to respect our own humanity before we can respect our brothers and sisters in the flesh. There were, however, other moments of high temptation when the road to power or preferment seemed open and the price of its attainment seemed ridiculously small.

There was a time in my career when I, like Bruno, was prominent in the debates of my times and wielded, for a while, more influence than was justified by my position or, indeed, my talent. I was president of the Australian Society of Authors.

I was one of the acknowledged leaders of the first teach-in at the Australian National University against our proposed commitment to the war in Vietnam. It was, and still is, one of the proud moments of my life when in July 1965 I stood before the assembly and made an affirmation that was published around the world:

> We are, most of us, citizens of a country in crisis—a crisis of armed involvement in South East Asia, whose outcome we cannot yet predict and whose consequences we shall not be able to determine for ourselves. Whatever these consequences may be, our children will inherit them. I submit to you, therefore, in all humility, that we have a clear duty, collectively and individually, to examine ourselves upon the nature of our involvement in Asia.
>
> It is our clear duty, as citizens of a democracy, to exercise our full right to call constantly to account those whom we have charged by ballot to conduct our affairs at home and our relations abroad.
>
> The which brings me, at one stride, to the main thesis of my talk. This is a political matter, a strategic matter. It is also a philosophic and moral matter and we will ignore this fact at our peril.
>
> I know that the Prime Minister has dismissed philosophy and morals from the argument with a stroke of his well-known wit and a wave of his paternal hand. He is the perfect pragmatist, who sees only the here and now. He is concerned with the fact, not with the idea.
>
> I would like to remind you that the idea is much, much more explosive than the fact. But I know as a simple fact that you do not wipe out a philosophy by dropping an atom bomb on Peking or a napalm bomb on a Vietnamese village. You will not wipe it out by extending this war into a human holocaust,

because out of the holocaust will arise a new, and perhaps more fearsome, dragon.

There were sequels to that first address: alienation of old friends and comrades in arms, who read my arguments as a kind of treachery; a concerted press campaign pushed hard by the then prime minister; threats against me and my family.

I was soon to learn another of the usances of power politics. Came the day when I was invited to lunch with the leader of the Labour Party in Australia and two or three of his colleagues. The lunch took place in the city branch of the Royal Prince Alfred Yacht Club, of which I was, and still am, a member. The proposal was made to me that I should join the Labour Party and that if I did I could look forward to rapid preferment within its ranks. I was, they told me, an eloquent proponent of its policy of nonintervention in Asia.

I was flattered by the offer. I promised to consider it. I went back home to my wife, Joy, and told her what had happened. Her reaction was swift and negative. Her words still ring in my ears: "My love, you have spent all your life trying to be a free man. Why would you want to put chains on yourself again? Join any party, and you will be bound, not by your own conscience, but by the creed of the party. Is that what you want?"

This is why I wrote *The Heretic,* a verse drama on Giordano Bruno that had its first performance at the Duke of York's Theatre in London's West End in 1969. It has been played many times since in other places. It has been transmitted on radio and television. I could not believe that any man should be required to sell his soul, however paltry a thing it might be—to anyone who promised him order, discipline, social acceptance, and three meals a day.

I wrote a play, because in a book it is all too easy to succumb to the treacherous balance of rationality. I wrote in verse, because I could express in no other way the turmoil in my own spirit. I wrote what I felt then and what I believe now: that a man has to know a reason for living and dying. The reason may be wrong, but his right to hold it in good faith is inalienable.

On the Writers' Walk in the forecourt of the Sydney Opera House, there is a series of bronze plaques dedicated to famous writers. I was privileged to have mine sited between Robert Louis Stevenson and Dame Mary Gilmore. The inscription I chose to identify myself was this quotation from *The Heretic:*

> . . . I claim
> No private lien on the truth, only
> A liberty to seek it, prove it in debate,
> And to be wrong a thousand times to reach
> A single rightness.

One other thing I have learned in a long lifetime is that language is a two-edged weapon. It can be used as freely in the service of tyranny as of liberty. It can be used to elevate and to debase, to tell a truth or promote a lie.

> Ever since the Greeks, we have been drunk
> With language! We have made a cage of words
> And shoved our God inside, as boys confine
> A cricket or a locust, to make him sing
> A private song! And look what great gob-stopping
> Words we use for God's simplicity,
> Hypostasis and homoousion!
> We burn men for these words—a baboon chatter
> Of human ignorance!—We burn men!

However, the argument goes much further. In a civilized society, error must be expressed as freely as truth, else how shall we distinguish one from the other? Liberty must be defended in flawed cases. Justice must be dispensed to those who seem least to merit it. The rights of the shabbiest persons must be those most strongly defended.

We must never forget that tyranny begins by a deliberate diminishment of dignity. The political prisoner is stripped before the interrogators. The function of the torturer is not only to hurt but to debase. The function of the propagandist is to create scapegoats by caricature.

As Bruno says in the play:

> It is not death I fear.
> Already I have died a dozen deaths
> Waiting for torture and the questioning.
> The terror that haunts me is quite different . . .
> They will make me a clown before I die!

The tragic matter is that all these evils are abetted and condoned by good men, for good causes: the stability of the State, doctrinal orthodoxy, traditional morality.

One of the men who signed the monstrous document of Bruno's condemnation was Cardinal Robert Bellamine, a canonized saint, known to his contemporaries as the meekest of men. How could he do it? I have thought often about this. I have come to the conclusion that institutional power distances men and women from their own humanity. They forget that men and women, not institutions, are the subjects and objects of salvation. The institutions may survive; people have only their precarious now. It is in the *now* that we are saved or damned. To legislate or adjudicate upon future consequences is one road to the terrible indifference of tyranny. It is for this reason that I put into the mouth of Giordano Bruno his final reply to the advocates who came to demand his second recantation in Rome:

Let us be clear!
This is what you ask: "Rejoin the flock,
Recite the Creeds. Deny what once you wrote,
Believing it was true. Then make an act
Of public penitence—we'll let you live!
Refuse, we will kill you!" That's the nub of it!
"Which of your gentlemen begot me? Which
Breathed into this sack of bones the life
I did not ask for? None of you? Who then?
Aldobrandini, who is now the Pope?
Did Bellarmino? Any cardinal
Of the Inquisitors? Who said to me,
A foetus in the womb, a puling babe,
"You have your life, but on the condition that
You thus believe"? No one! Not even God!
So, gentlemen, I say you have no right
To make terms for my life. I tell you then—
No! I will not recant. I will not sign!

There is an addendum to this speech that, according to the
few surviving records of the Roman trial, are the words uttered
by Bruno when sentence was pronounced upon him:

At this moment, gentlemen, I think
That you are more afraid of me than I
Of you.

CHAPTER 9

THE MAKING
of PROPHECY

I would like to remind you that prophecy—the expression of care and concern in the assembly—is one of the most ancient charismata. It is, I regret to say, one of those that has fallen into disuse, has been rendered suspect and sometimes suppressed within the Church.

In a canonical sense, I have no patent to teach within the Church. In truth, however, I am a sharer in the priesthood of believers. I can administer baptism, the sacrament of initiation. I am charged to express Christ and to spread his good news through my own life. If I fail in example—as I often have—if I falsify the message—as, believe me, I have tried never to do— then I am responsible under God.

However, this is not the only brief I hold. I am an aging pilgrim, one of the elders who has been a long time on the road. I have experience to share. You have the freedom to reject it as a graybeard's babbling, but I have the liberty and the right and, in this case, I believe, the duty to speak out, to make prophesy in the assembly.

Before I go further, let me make in clear terms the affirmation that sustains us all. I believe in the working of the Holy Spirit within the visible and invisible assembly of the people of God. I believe that the Spirit, like the wind, blows where it will and that we act most foolishly when we try to plot or determine the action of the Spirit. I will go further and say that when we—any of us, high or low in the assembly of the faithful—try to set limits on the saving action of the Spirit, we commit misfeasance as Christians.

I am sad for what I see happening in the community of which I have been all my life a member. I say this not in despair but in regret for the good folk, old and young, who are being lost to us, who are losing hope and belief in the relevance of the gospel message. For that, we their elders are in part to blame. In part, also, those who rule the Church are to blame because they have in many instances chosen authority over charity, because their legalistic approach to human life alienates our brothers and sisters and disfigures the familial image of the Church.

I am reminded of a passage in the Gospel of Saint John:

> The scribes and pharisees brought to Jesus a woman taken in adultery. . . . They said to him "Rabbi, this woman was even now taken in adultery. Moses and the law commanded us to stone such a one. What do you say?" Jesus said nothing. They continued to question him. Then he lifted his head and said to them: "He that is without sin among you let him cast the first stone." And again he stooped down and wrote on the ground. The others hearing this went out one by one, beginning at the eldest. Jesus remained alone with the woman. Then he said to her: "Woman, where are those who accuse you?" The woman said: "There is no-one, Lord." And Jesus said: "Neither will I condemn you. Go now and sin no more."

I have always thought of that as a particularly eerie moment in the gospel narrative. The old-fashioned commentary used to be that Jesus wrote the sins of the accusers. That has always seemed to me to be an unnecessary embellishment as well as an impossibly long catalog. My own guess is that he doodled, scribbled nonsense symbols as an act of contempt for these so clever and so cruel hypocrites. In any case, it is the only record of Jesus ever writing anything. The first scurry of wind blew it away, or perhaps he scuffed it out with his own sandal. Who knows?

The irony for me is that we who follow him have erected whole mountains of books over his simple teaching. We have written and sometimes forged whole volumes of decretals and canons and acts of the apostolic see and admonitions and anathemas and condemnations of death and excommunications of whole peoples, and we have called it—what?—the exercise of the magisterium, the exercise of the power of the keys.

Let me remind you, however, that, exercising the same power, we tortured and burned men and women, too, for alleged heresy, sorcery, and witchcraft.

I confess to you that the older I get, the more I am haunted by the contrasts between the two images: the dark man from Nazareth bowed over the temple pavement, scribbling in the dust, and the huge and fearsome array of hierarchies and legislators and inquisitors down the centuries entrenched behind their mountains of documents, demanding, as the price of faith, obedience to their magistracy.

The contrast creates a nightmare for many: a nightmare of alienation from Christ's own simple summary: *"By this shall all men know that you are my disciples, that you have love for one another."* I tell you now in the cold light of observable fact what I predicted when I first returned to my homeland fourteen years ago: we are in schism, a schism of indifference, because those who regulate the Church have committed themselves to a policy of sterile legalism, a historic *romanita—Roman-ness—* instead of a policy of loving care to inform it and revivify it with the saving Spirit of its master.

On this point, let me interpolate. Here is a passage written by Archbishop Elias Zoghby, vice patriarch of the Melchite Church, whose intervention in Vatican Council II on behalf of the Eastern rites in the Church was both powerful and productive. He speaks in this passage of the differences between East and West in the interpretation and administration of marriage laws.

> We must admit that there does exist an ecclesiastical tradition of tolerance, clear and venerable like every other tradition of the Church which was accepted and practised by many holy fathers of the East and of the West. The East has always followed this tradition of tolerance and has remained faithful to it. The West maintained it for many centuries with the positive approval of many of its Bishops, Popes and Councils and, in fact, never attempted to condemn it in the East after the cessation of its practice in the West.

Love has been lost to us. *Res ipse loquitur*—The facts speak for themselves. Those among you who are pastors see your congregations declining and the numbers of aspirants, men and women, to vocations in religious life declining also. Those of you who are parents are troubled because your children seem to find the moral and religious message of the Church irrelevant to their needs or alienating in their lives.

I was in Rome during the wonderful, hopeful years of Vatican Council II. Since then, I have seen the progress that was then begun—which I saw and still see as a progress of charity within the Church—grind to a halt. I have seen, on the other hand, the processes of alienation quicken and more and more people standing outside the doors of the Church, which seem closed against them because the cost of reentry seems beyond their strength and the grace beyond their reach.

In a very strange way, it seems to me that the role of authority within the Church has been distorted. The exercise of authority is not, and cannot be, a self-determining, self-sufficing act like the act of creation. The only justification of the *magisterium* is as a function of *ministerium,* of service to souls who are the subjects and objects of salvation. To use a very ancient and primitive symbol, we are not the makers of fire, we are the carriers of fire for the tribe that does not know how to make it. On too many occasions in history, the keepers of fire have turned into tyrants or cold-hearted conservators of that which they do not own.

We, the Church, whether as a hierarchic institution or as a familial body, do not confer the gift of faith. That is the direct gift of God. We accept the profession of faith. We confer the sacrament of initiation, but faith is not in our gift. We should remember that. All those in authority should remember that with great respect in all our dealings with one another.

That which the faithful find hardest to forgive is the unwillingness of their senior pastors to confront openly with them the problems they face in the world as it is today.

Let us be very clear; not all the enactments of popes or sacred congregations have been, or are, good, wise, or even just. In the Church, as in civil life, bad law brings the principle of law into disrepute. Dubious law puts the principle in doubt. Law imposed upon people without explanation, with its processes loaded against them *ab initio,* is of its very nature an injustice. A law beyond effective appeal is a tyranny.

Why do I make so much of this? Because at this moment in this pontificate, the Church is being governed by two negatives and a positive. The two negatives are *non expedit* (it is not expedient) and *non e opportuno* (it is not timely). The positive is *fiat* (let it be done thus). In this kind of regulatory climate, there are no relatives. Everything is absolute. We even have a huge catechism, like a lexicon of good and evil, to which you can refer but from which the reasons of the heart seem conspicuously absent.

In today's Church, papal teaching on birth control is regarded by the majority of the faithful as, at best, a directive that is dubious in theology and, at worst, an arbitrary exercise of the magisterium.

The question of a celibate clergy falls into the untimely category.

The content and administration of and the theology behind the marriage laws of the Church are all questionable, and this, the most critical, the most divisive, and the least just of all Church legislation, is the one that receives the least public attention from authority in Rome. There are many other solutions than those provided in existing canons, but they are not being addressed and, in some cases, are being positively impeded by Rome.

The question of women clergy is closed. So, men and women of goodwill are now in the position of having either to remain silent on deeply held convictions or to make a public challenge, not only against a determination but against the person of a reigning pontiff.

I will not make that challenge in this context. I will simply remind you that, in the context of Church history, the greatest stain upon our reputation as conservators of the gospel truth has been that it takes us decades and centuries to admit our mistakes and that it is only God who can repair the damage they have caused. I do, however, have to raise with you the big question as to whether the magistracy of the Church has the right for any issue of law or discipline to deny to the people of God their access to the saving word and to the channels of grace.

I submit that we should expect more from our hierarchy than hoary platitudes about the grace of God being sufficient to us all if only we cooperate with it. To me, an elderly man standing on the ridge and looking across the dark valley into eternity, the only answer is a continuous dispensation of love and the tolerances of love.

We live at the heart of a dark mystery—a tooth-and-claw creation made, we say, by a loving God. Saved, we say, by a crucified redeemer.

The visible fact of the matter is that the world for millions is a sad, sorry, and a mad place and Christ himself had to plead the ignorance of those who were crucifying him.

I do not deny the principle of authority as a necessary element of the ministry of support and love that holds any community together. I do warn in the strongest terms that the imprudent or misguided or arbitrary misuse of authority will only increase the present alienation of the Catholic community and of those who are their brothers and sisters in spirit in other communions and, indeed, other religions.

In some strange and frightening fashion, the traffic of communication within our Church has for a long time now been on a one-way street from the heights to the plains where the people live. More and more Catholics, men and women, are better educated than some of their pastors. They know better how the world wags and how great are the needs of ordinary people. It is they who sustain the charities that still affirm our common humanity, but their voices are not heard. Catholic newspapers and religious programs on television and radio are distressingly bland and correspondingly irrelevant. Pastoral reports and the reports of nuncios to Rome are filtered and colored. Who, we ask ourselves sometimes, who but God hears the cry of the beggar at the gates?

Let me remind you of a passage I wrote as far back as 1959 in *The Devil's Advocate*. The Bishop of Valenta is addressing Blaise Meredith:

> The Church is a theocracy ruled by a priestly caste of which you and I are members. We have a language of our own—a hieratic language if you like—formal, stylised, admirably adapted to legal and theological definition. Unfortunately, we also have a rhetoric of our own which like the rhetoric of the politician says much and conveys little. But we are not politicians, we are teachers, teachers of a truth which we claim to be essential to man's salvation. Yet how do we preach it? We talk roundly of faith and hope as if we were making a fetishist's incantation. What is faith? A blind leap into the hands of God. An inspired act of will which is our only answer to the terrible mystery of where we came from and where we are going. What is hope? A child's trust in the hand that will lead it out of the terrors that reach from the dark. We preach love and fidelity as if these were teacup tales, not bodies writhing on a bed and hot words in dark places and souls tormented by loneliness. We talk to the people every Sunday but our words do not reach them because we have forgotten our mother tongue.

And, lest it be thought that my plea is too personal, my attitude too subjective, let me recall to you the final article in the code of canon law: *"In ecclesia suprema lex salus animarum"*— "In the community of the faithful the supreme law is the welfare of souls."

We have to ask, and we have the right and the duty to ask, how far, in today's Church, that supreme law has been breached by expedient policy or by the exaggerated use of authority. Let us never forget the unwritten codicil to the assumption of papal power: That no pontiff, however much a reformer he may be, will directly countermand or contradict the prescriptions of his predecessors. There will be no rehabilitation of even permissible ideas by the successor to the present pontiff, whoever he may be. Change will be allowed to happen. It will not be *made* to happen. The fear of damage to the teaching and governing authority will override everything.

Which brings me by a round turn to a primary question. What do I see as the future of the Catholic Church?

In the short term, under the present pontificate, I believe that the same trends will continue. The schism of indifference will spread. The number of candidates for service in religious and priestly life will continue to decline. Expressions of disagreement and contention within the body of the faithful will continue. There will be a massive protest by women and a continuing alienation of women from the celibate oligarchy by which the Church is presently ruled. We will see more and more examples of two differing phenomena within the Church. The first is the emergence of more and more rigorist groups, louder and more emphatic in their professions of allegiance to the ancient ways of the Church, by which it seems that many understand only what happened after the Council of Trent.

On the other hand, we shall see charismatic groups, expressing the enthusiasm of even earlier times in prayer groups, in brotherly and sisterly associations within the congregation. But the deep hurt and division within the Church will still remain within the post–Vatican II generation, who will see the fading of the hopes they had invested in the updating and renewal of the Church. They will continue their tillage of whatever part of the vineyard they work in, but some of the heart will be gone from them and they will wear the Church, not with the joy of the children of God but like a penitential hair shirt. Meantime, by the mere fact of shortage of vocations, the faithful will be distanced still further from the ministry of the word and of the sacrament.

How then will renewal come, because come it must? Even popes and curial cardinals are mortal. There are disagreements and dissensions in every one of the corridors of power, however hushed they may be, however softly the dissension is expressed. So, I ask again, how will renewal come? I have to say what I said at the beginning: I believe in the power of the Spirit. I do not know, I cannot predict, how the Spirit may express itself to renew the life of faith and hope and, most important of all, charity within the community.

I believe, though I cannot prove, that there will come a surge of power from women within the Church, more and more of whom are highly trained educators, philosophers, and theologians, more and more of whom will give challenge to patriarchal mind-sets—as Saint Catherine of Siena, a girl in her early twenties, once gave challenge to and heaped moral reproach upon the delinquent papacy in Avignon. There was a martial vigor in what she urged upon Gregory XI: *Siatemi uomo virile e non timoroso*—Be for me a virile man and not a coward.

I shall not be here to see the renewal, though I hope for it and pray for it and give my testimony on the crying need for it.

It is not my wish that the testimony should incite dissension but rather that it should lead to a *curative communion* between those high and low in the Church, who are all in the end brothers and sisters under the skin.

If each of us were locked in a silent room, deprived of all sensory reference, we should very soon become disoriented and, finally, insane. The person who would probably endure longest would be the one who was practiced in withdrawal, in meditation, whose life had an outside reference to God. The fact is, you see, that we live only in communion—not only with our present but with the past and the future as well. We are haunted by a whole poetry of living, by lullabies half remembered and the sounds of train whistles in the night and the scent of lavender in a summer garden. We are haunted by grief, too, and fear and images of childhood terror and the macabre dissolutions of age. But I am sure—and this is the nub of my testimony—that it is in this domain of our innermost daily lives that the Holy Spirit establishes his own communion with us. This is how the gift is given that we call grace: the sudden illumination, the sharp regret that leads to penitence or forgiveness, the opening of the heart to the risk of love. Authority is irrelevant here. Authority is the one-eyed man in the kingdom of the blind. It can command us to everything except love and understanding. So what am I trying to tell you? Peter is dead and Paul is dead and James the brother of the Lord. Their dust is blown away by the winds of centuries. Were they large men, little men, fair or dark? Who knows? Who cares? The testimony of the Spirit made through them still endures: *"Though I speak with the tongues of men and of angels and have not charity, I am become like a sounding brass or a tinkling cymbal."*

CHAPTER 10

DIPTYCH:

MEMORIAL *of* TWO POPES

The first of these memorials, the obituary of Pope John XXIII, was written in June 1963. The second, entitled *Reflections on a Papal Occasion*, was written thirty-two years later to mark the visit of Pope John Paul II to Australia for the beatification of Mother Mary MacKillop, founder of the Josephite Sisters.

I present them together in this volume because of the extraordinary differences in my personal circumstances in each case and the difference in my personal attitude.

In 1963 I was still under censure because of my second marriage outside the Church. I did, however, attend Mass with my family as a public evidentiary protest against the decision of an ecclesiastical marital court. I did not, however, take the sacraments, even when my small daughter made her first communion. I was, nevertheless, filled with what I recall as an extraordinary joy and a deep peace during the pontificate of the good Pope John. He had thrown open the windows of the Church to fresh thinking, to fresh approaches in charity and compassion to our diverse and troubled human family. I was waiting for justice. Now I was prepared to wait in hope.

The second piece was written in my seventy-ninth year, when I was living no longer under censure. My marriage had been validated by the Church, and I was once again sharing in its sacramental life. I was also an old man. I was conscious that whatever judgments I made, I would have to account for on my own judgment day. If I perverted the truth, the perversion would haunt me through what was left of my life. There was, as the reader will discern, little joy in my second memorial. There was peace, yes, hard-won but rock-solid. There was also concern—deep concern—with what we had lost from the community of the faithful and what we still stand to lose.

I believe I can say with certainty that I remained in communion with the Church, even when the Church itself excluded me, and I remain there still, principally because of the presence of John XXIII, the good pastor, whom I never met, though I did meet his predecessor and his successor. Goodness went out from this man to me. I acknowledged it then. I acknowledge it again, now.

You will read the two memorials and make your own judgments. Both were written from the heart.

Builder of Bridges for Us Poor Devils: Pope John XXIII

I am very close to tears as I begin to set down these words. What can I say of a man so manifestly good, so manifestly the victim—or is it the victor—in a drama of divine irony whose poignant prayer as he lies stricken is not for the salvation of his own soul but for the salvation of a work begun in the name of God?

I have no dignity in the Church. I have no personal merit to commend me for the task of writing a eulogy, save perhaps this—that I am, in the spirit, a stumbling son of Angelo Giuseppe Roncalli. And, as a son, I want to say what his living and the thought of his dying have meant to me and to other souls still vagrant on this puzzling planet.

I live twelve thousand miles from Rome. I stand with hundreds of millions of other believers on the lowest level of the complex hierarchic order of the Church; but I wander widely and I am troubled by the spectacle of misery and poverty, and injustice and oppression, and the million faces of despair. I wrestle daily with the mystery of how all this could have issued, as the Christian faith affirms it does, from the single creative act of an all-good and all-knowing Divinity.

To me Angelo Roncalli presented himself always as a man who carried the burden of the same mystery, who shared the agony that it imposes on the human spirit, who knew the wild and risky leap demanded by the act of faith—and who knew, too, from how many millions the grace to make it has been withheld.

From the day of his election the makers of legends were busy about him. Even they could not obscure the true nature of this man—shrewd, pragmatic, kindly, too simple to be seduced by eminence, too gregarious to be happy in the baroque enclave of Vatican City, a man with a sense of fraternity and a gift of compassion which even the formalities of Vatican communication could not distort.

The Romans named him *un Papa simpatico*. And everyone wished he were younger, so that the imprint of his personality might be deeper on the corporate life of the Church and the common life of the world. We had had a surfeit of princes and politicians and theologians—even of conventional saints. We needed a man who spoke the language of the heart, who understood that the dialogue of God with man is carried on in terms far different from the semantics of professional philosophers. We have had him too briefly.

Many of my generation felt that the traditional relationship between clergy and the people had become defective. We acknowledged without reservation the dignity of the priestly office, its divine function in the renewal of the sacrificial act and in the dispensation of sacramental grace. We respected the abnegation and dedication imposed by the celibate state. We supported our pastors according to their needs and our capacities. We built schools and monasteries and hospitals. We financed missions and works of charity. We carried double and triple burdens to educate our children in the faith.

But many of us felt, not without reason, that there was too much emphasis on the *magisterium* of the hierarchy—their authority as moral arbiters, interpreters of dogma and administrators of the temporal structure of the Church. We felt that there was not enough understanding of their *ministerium*—the service of the Creator through and by spiritual and temporal service rendered to the people.

In half a generation the vista of the universe had exploded into galactic dimensions. The human spirit was being submitted to monstrous tensions—moral, political, economic. And while we clung desperately to the deposit of faith, we longed for a renewal of the intellectual and pastoral life of the Church so that we might live—through the faith—hopefully and actively in the world into which we were born.

We were not cenobites. We were men of the Twentieth Century and we could not opt out of it. We were not only members of a church, we were members of the diverse human family as well and we could not opt out of that either. It was like the breaking of a new day when we heard the call of John XXIII for an *aggiornamento*—for an updating of the Church, her manners, her customs and her interpretation of the deposit of faith into the language of this millennial century.

When John XXIII was elected Pontiff, he abrogated nothing of the primacy of his office. Yet one of his first acts was to make himself more readily available to his brother bishops. Later he intervened in the debates of the Ecumenical Council and in the lobbies of its members to affirm that the Roman Curia was not the Pope, and that the Pope was brother to every bishop in Christendom and servant of every human soul in the world.

Of all the recent Popes, it seems that John XXIII was the least afraid of schism, of heresy or of the militancy of non-Christian religions. A man of simple faith, he believed in the indwelling of the Holy Spirit and in the promise of perpetuity made by Christ to the Church. He put no store in interdict or excommunication because he was also a man of simple charity who understood that, although human beings are limited by God's covenant with them, God Himself is not so limited. He knew that all men must live with the burdens and confusions of their own history, and that salvation or damnation hangs, in the last resort, upon God's judgment of the final direction of a man's will—toward Him or away from Him. He claimed without reservation his right as the supreme pastor to preach truth and refute error, but he gave the impression of a man ready at all times to suspend judgment on human confusion and human delinquency. All other Pontiffs knew these things—preached them, too. What has made John XXIII so different is his lively and intimate sense of their application to the commerce of life, immortally reflected in *Pacem in Terris,* his encyclical on peace.

I am chary of miracles; but I think there has been a kind of miracle in the way Pope John managed to impress his charity upon the Church and upon the world. Most people have seen him only in photographs. His own voice has not often been heard. Mainly his words filtered out to the faithful through newspaper reports and the variant voices of preachers, good and bad. But somehow we have all felt him, and felt that God was with him. In his hands the crosier of the bishop has meant what it was meant to mean—the crook of the kindly Shepherd, to whom the wayworn and the stragglers meant more than those penned safely in the sheepfold.

When he was elected Pope, he became heir to a long list of titles: Bishop of Rome, Vicar of Jesus Christ, Successor of the Prince of the Apostles, Supreme Pontiff of the Universal Church, Patriarch of the West, Primate of Italy, Archbishop and Metropolitan of the Roman Province, Sovereign of the Vatican City State. Yet the title which has seemed to sit most comfortably on him is that of Pontifex: the builder of bridges. He goes too soon and he leaves his work unfinished, but the bridges he planned are already abuilding—bridges of understanding and tolerance between the separated families of Christendom and the nations of East and West.

The formula on which he based all his architecture was very simple: "I have tried to preserve my calm and balance while investigating and evaluating things and persons about me, ever concerned more with that which unites than with that which divides."

He was never a polemical man. He disliked contention and preferred to rely upon discussion and persuasive prompting rather than to invoke the authority of his office. He ordered that even the admonitions and censures of the Holy Office be couched in moderate language so that men of good will might have room to move through the most risky speculations to a fuller understanding of the truth. He was never a political man. He was a diplomat long enough to know that political action creates more problems than it solves.

There was a great boldness in his planning, a devastating directness. He encouraged the most daring speculations of modern theology and he lent the weight of his influence to those ecumenical dialogues which aimed at breaking down semantic and historic barriers between Catholic and non-Catholic theologians.

There are some in the Church who were disappointed because he did not take a more militant line against Russian Communism, there are some who were shocked because he accepted birthday greetings from the premier of Russia and then received his son-in-law in private audience. Yet this incident illuminated his whole attitude to the affairs of human souls. He knew that every society and every system survives by virtue of what is good in it, just as human beings are kept from the ultimate madness of despair by that in their nature which is good and conformable to a divine pattern.

John XXIII has left us: a great man, and a great Pope. For this very reason there is rare tragedy in his passing. The tragedy is that, having begun so much, he will not be permitted to see the fruits of his labour; he has seen only the first faint buds. Yet in this, as in all else, his life has been patterned on that of the Christ whose vicar he was. He has walked for all too short a time, scattering the seeds of truth and charity on good ground and stony soil, and has endured the painful crucifixion of illness and frustration. Now, at the end, he must abandon himself and all his unfinished work into the hands of God.

How has he felt during these last months, perched on his lonely eminence with the world spread beneath him like a campaign map and above him the monstrous mystery of the Godhead? There must have been times when his aged shoulders bent under the burden and even his stout peasant heart quailed at the thought of things undone. Even the mercy of death was delayed for him—as it was for his Master.

History will be kind to him, I think, because he has been a kindly man who had compassion on the multitudes, "seeing them harried and abject like sheep that have no shepherd."

Princes and priests are mourned as rarely as they are thanked, but many will weep for this one because he has been, in truth, what he was named to be: a servant of the servants of God.

Will they canonize him and make him, officially, a saint in the calendar? In a way I hope not. For my part, I do not want to see him idealized by a Vatican painter, lit by a thousand candles in St. Peter's, reproduced in plaster and gilt and sold to pious pilgrims. I want to remember him for what he has been—a loving man, a simple priest, a good pastor and a builder of bridges across which we poor devils may hope one day to scramble to salvation.

Reflections on a Papal Occasion:
Pope John Paul II

The Australian visit of His Holiness Pope John Paul II was scored in a triumphant major key, appropriate to a great national occasion. His Holiness listed in the calendar of the Blessed a battling local lady, Mother Mary MacKillop. His official confirmation of her heriot virtue inflated our national pride. It affirmed—at least to the faithful—that we could excel not only in sport and science and the arts, but in the more exacting disciplines of the spiritual life. It provided a welcome respite from the sad scandals which bedevilled the Roman Catholic community in this country and elsewhere.

The burden of the Papal message was predictable: *"Lift up your hearts! God's in his heaven, Father, Son and Holy Ghost. God's saints still walk the earth. Lo! Here is one, named for Christ's mother, who in her pilgrimage of service glorified God in her womanhood!"*

The message delivered, His Holiness went back to the Vatican: his own Gethsemane, the garden of his private agony where the vista opens to a restless and divided Church, a threatening world full of violence, with the Hill of Crucifixion looming dark against a blood-red sky.

Like all of us, the Pope owes God a death. He seems to be working with compulsive haste to set his stewardship in order so that he can meet this final demand. It is late in the day for him. He is seventy-four years old. He has held for sixteen years the most complex and least rewarding office in the world. At the time of his election he was a vigorous, athletic man. He chose for himself the role of a travelling pastor circling the globe to proclaim the Good News in person to the scattered Churches. He was maimed by an assassin's bullet. Now he is obviously ailing—ill-conditioned, one would think, for yet another long-haul flight, another round of ceremonies and speeches.

It is a long time now, since Leo X, the Medici Pope, was able to announce to his cronies: *"Since God has given us the Papacy, let us enjoy it."* In this day and age, the office of Pontiff imposes brute labour, the solitude of absolute authority and the practical impossibility of rescinding any mistake. The legendary secrecy of the Vatican provides small protection from the spotlight of daily media scrutiny. It is at best a gossamer garment, torn in many places, which reveals much more than it conceals.

Even so, the traditional Roman comedy still plays itself out, with sedulous stage-management. The setting is grandiose and the title a little old-fashioned. It is called *The Management of Princes.* The Theme is very simple: how you elect a man to absolute power and then limit his use of it. Even so tough and hard-headed a man as John Paul II is not proof against the endless exactions of the performance. There are, after all, only twenty-four hours in his day. He has only so much human fabric to spend.

Small wonder then that he has the look of an old warrior, girding himself for one more battle, which he knows he must fight, but cannot win.

He has never been an innocent in the strategies of power, political or religious. How could he be? In his student youth he was trained in the necessary conspiracies of survival, first under German occupation, then under the Russians and later under a Marxist administration. He learnt early that to hold a resistance movement together one had to exercise authority—to confront overt power with covert strength. The final result was a spectacular victory, the beginning of the end of the Russian Marxist hegemony in Europe. It is only five years since Poland held its first free elections in half a century.

To many, it seems that a resurgent Poland, one in race and faith, may be the 20th century paradigm of St. Augustine's city of God where church and state plough the parallel furrows of religion and politics for the betterment of the people of God. Those who cherish this vision accredit Pope John Paul II as "an unassailable moral authority, the Greatest Pole of All Time."

Others see it differently. They worry about the proposed Concordat between the Vatican and the Polish Government. They see it as a step towards a new quasi-religious state in which the clergy will be confirmed once again as a privileged caste. As one recent commentator put it:

"Now the danger is . . . the assumption that choice is actually the greatest source of human misery. The grey mass of humanity isn't ready for it. Consequently it is the obligation of the Great and the Good to take away the options and free people from the unhappy obligations of making the choice."

These are Polish points of view but they are specific to Pope John Paul himself. It was inevitable that, given the success of his tactics in his homeland, he should try to apply them to the universal church. It was also inevitable that in the big, wide, plural world, they would fail. The hard fact is that, with the curial advisers and spokesmen he has chosen for himself, the Pontiff has painted himself into a corner.

He will not surrender the legal power bases he has already retaken: the discretions he has subtracted from his brother Bishops, to vest in himself and in the *dicasteries,* the central administrative bodies in Rome. For him, collegiality was always too great a risk—or was it, one asks without malice, too great a leap of faith in the pervasive working of the Spirit among the people of God.

His problem, however, goes much further than empowerment in ministry. In matters of doctrine—which are the credal summaries of the developing revelation of eternal mysteries—he has put himself in the position where he can no longer publicly countenance reasonable doubt or encourage legitimate alternative opinion.

In too many matters of doctrine and of law, certainty has been prescribed by magisterial authority: a dangerous and alienating exercise for men and women of goodwill, who still stand, dirty and bloody in the arena.

Whatever their shortcomings, they still confess the faith. They cling to the hope of salvation. They cry out for the dispensation of healing charity. They have the right to require from all their pastors an accounting and an explanation of the obediences and the interpretations imposed upon them. They ask why no one listens to them, why no one reasons with them as our Lord reasoned with his disciples in their puzzlements over his teachings.

They wonder, sometimes, what has happened to that oldest and most honourable of all pastoral titles—Servant of the Servants of God. One thing they do understand very clearly: that they are the Church, the Pilgrim People of God. Without them the words of life would be lost in empty air.

They are painfully aware that, under this Pontificate, dissenters have been silenced and open debate on contentious but vital issues has been prorogued. They know that the close counsellors of the Pontiff and his spokesmen in Rome are of a rigorist cast. They know that he has hand-picked many of the senior hierarchy and most of his own cabinet, the College of Cardinals, who will also elect his successor.

In all this, the Pontiff has shown himself to be the most pragmatic of leaders—if not always the most sensitive to the human condition. Yet, like him or not, praise him or damn him, he has always hewn to the line he has drawn on the timber. The faithful, wryly wise in their collective experience, try to suspend a final judgment. Some of them quote hopefully: "There's a divinity that shapes our ends, rough-hew them how we will. . . ."

Let me interpolate here a personal comment. I have a special feeling about this Pontiff. I have a sympathy for the burden he carries. I have at least an elementary understanding of the dilemmas of his office.

I was first accredited to the Vatican in 1958 on special assignment for the *Daily Mail* of London. I lived for seven years in Rome in regular contact with all ranks and conditions of the prelacy. The experiences of those years were recorded in three novels and two films made in and around the Vatican. I have, therefore, some knowledge of how the place works and how it works upon the man who wears the Fisherman's ring. The words I wrote thirty-two years ago still hold good:

> The Papacy is the most paradoxical office in the world, the most absolute and yet the most limited. . . . The man who holds it claims divine guarantee against error, yet is less assured of salvation than the meanest of his subjects. The keys of the Kingdom dangle at his belt, yet he can find himself locked out forever from the Peace of Election and the Communion of

saints. . . . If he does not walk sometimes in terror and pray often in darkness, then he is a fool.

As I recall these lines, I find myself slipping back into the novelist's habit of seeking analogies between himself and his subject: verifiable similarities which may ultimately give life and authenticity to the fictional portrait. But we are not talking fiction here. We are talking fact.

There is a clearly defined relationship between Morris West of Sydney Town and His Holiness Pope John Paul II, Vicar of Christ, successor to the Prince of the Apostles. We were made brothers in the same Baptism. He was elected to be my Spiritual Father in Christ. That gives him an authority over me, and me great claims on him. He enacts and administers laws, some good, some highly defective, which touch me and my children and their children.

Beyond these precise relationships, there are similarities also. We are contemporaries. I am in fact four years older than he. We were both educated in the same strict religious climate— the stormy afterglow of Pius X and his anathemas against modernism. I was trained as a teaching Brother in the Christian schools, he was educated to be a priest; but the climate of our early religious schooling was almost identical. The only difference was that I was brought up among the Irish, who in matters of religion and politics were just as stubborn, just as intolerant of dissent, just as long rememberers, just as peremptory in judgment as the Poles.

We survived the same war, he in occupied Poland, I in the South Pacific. We have, I would guess, experienced the same frustrations at the diminution of our strength by age and infirmity. We are both impatient men who do not suffer fools gladly; though I think it may have been easier for me than for him to arrive at tolerance and understanding. I can grow old among my grandchildren while he will be locked, until he dies, in the bleak solitude of power, becoming more dependent every day upon the counsels, good or bad, of those whom he has raised to office.

But we are joined by more than this. Fifteen years before the event, I wrote a novel, which proved, in part at least, to be a prophecy. It was called *The Shoes of the Fisherman* and it dealt with the election of a Slavic Pope, Kiril I. Even today, I cannot quite understand some of the uncanny presciences which were associated with the book, which is still in publication around the world. What I can say is that the work was inspired by the words of John XXIII: *"Let us seek that which unites us and not that which divides."*

I was echoing this thought when I put into the mouth of my fictional Kiril the following words:

> The strangest story in the Old Testament is the story of Jacob who wrestled with the angel and conquered him and forced him to tell his name. But Jacob came away from the struggle limping. I, too, am a limping spirit. I have felt reason and the foundations of my faith rock in the dark bunker and under the lights and the relentless inquisition. I believe still. I am committed more completely than ever before to the Deposit of Faith; but I am no longer prepared to say, "God is thus, man is thus," and make an end of it. Wherever I turn on this high pinnacle, I am confronted with mystery. I believe in the Godly harmony which is the result of the eternal creative act; but I do not always hear the harmony. I must wrestle with the cacophony and apparent discord of the score, knowing that I shall not hear the final grand resolution until the day I die and, hopefully, am united with God.

It is precisely in this sense of a shared mystery that many in the Church feel alienated today by and from the man who is their Supreme Pastor. His utterances—and those of the curial officials who speak in his name—seem often too curt, too peremptory, too dispassionate in reasoning, too poor in compassion, to give comfort or light on the darkling pilgrim road. As one distinguished educator—a longtime nun—put it to me recently: *"They talk at us and about us; but they don't listen. And who in a patriarchal hierarchy understands women anyway? They leave us very lonely."*

The sense of exclusion from common counsel, of being subjects and objects of pastoral direction instead of sharers in familial love plagues us all. The gap between pastors and people has grown wider every day since Vatican II. Every restriction on open discussion widens it still more. It is a far cry back to the original invitation of Jesus: *"Come to me all you who labour and are heavily burdened and I will refresh you. . . . My yoke is sweet and my burden is light."*

This alienation is part of the Pontiff's burden too. The idiom of his style of government belies his own compassion. I have watched him in close-up through the eye of a movie camera during the rituals of Holy Week in Rome: the washing of the feet on Maundy Thursday, the Stations of the Cross in the Colosseum on Good Friday. These are more than ceremonies, they are figurations of Christ himself in the last days of his life. The face which was recorded on our film was that of a suffering man, full of unexpressed anguish. For those moments, the Vicar of Christ seemed to wear the face of Christ himself, the "Man of Sorrows acquainted with infirmity."

In truth, he has much cause for grief. His world, which is our world, too, seems to be spinning out of control. The signs of the times read like the apocalyptic warning: *"wars and rumours of wars, famines and earthquakes in diverse places."* His Church is distressed, discouraged and deeply ashamed of its own very public defects.

On the other hand, it is surfeited with reproaches, admonitions and repressions. It waits, like the men and women and children of Israel, parched in the desert, for the Man with the Staff to strike the rock and release the living waters of charity, compassion and reconciliation.

We are told that a second miracle will be needed to raise Mother Mary MacKillop to the status of a full-grown saint. Maybe this is the miracle we should all pray for.

CHAPTER 11

THE LAZARUS SYNDROME

I've always wondered about Lazarus. He had walked through
the gates of death. Did he want to return to life? Did he thank Jesus
for bringing him back? What kind of man was he afterwards?
How did the world look to him?

—Morris West, *Lazarus*

The calendar told me I was in my seventy-second year,
so I knew I was getting old. I took it for granted that
stairs were steeper, hills were higher, that it took twice
as much effort to get out of a chair, to walk to my postbox, to
write a paragraph of prose.

I had always promised myself that I would try to grow old
gracefully. So, I didn't make too much of a fuss about the occasional chest pains, the increasing breathlessness, and the long
dozes over my desk. I did, however, resolve—with a certain
amount of pressure from my wife—that as soon as I'd finished
my book I would have my yearly checkup, take more exercise,
shed some weight. Thus and thus.

I kept the promise. My local G.P. gave me an electrocardio-
gram, did the usual tests, agreed that I was out of condition,
but assured me that "for a man of my age" I wasn't really in bad
shape. However, just as a precaution, he would recommend me
to a cardiac specialist for further tests. That didn't bother me
too much. The specialist was a neighbor and friend. I'd visited

him before. He'd always reassured me: the stress tests weren't bad "for a man of my age"; if I lost some weight and did some exercise, I'd almost make the geriatric team at the Olympics!

This visit was no exception. "For a man of my age" in a sedentary occupation, I wasn't in bad shape. However—this was almost an afterthought—just as an extra precaution, he would put me into hospital for an angiogram. It would be a simple procedure. I would go in at nine and be out at five.

An angiogram is a procedure by which a catheter is passed into the arterial system so that its course can be plotted and photographed. It's done while you're mildly sedated, and if you're fond of home movies, you can even watch the whole thing happening on a monitor screen. There are, however, more interesting spectator sports. Most interesting to me was my friend's final promise: "I'm betting twenty to one we'll find everything clean. I'll see you at four in the afternoon with the results. After that, you can go home."

Punctually at four, there he was, perched on the foot of my bed, asking me the joke question: "Which do you want first, the good news or the bad news?" I told him I'd prefer to get the bad out of the way and then savor the good. He gave it to me cold turkey.

"You've got less than five percent function on the left side of your heart. You're a candidate for a massive heart attack that will most probably kill you. It can happen any day."

He took out his prescription pad and made a rough sketch showing what would happen when a small blood clot blocked the narrowed arteries. Then he gave me the good news.

"You're a walking time bomb; but we can defuse you. We'll do a double bypass, replacing the diseased arteries with a vein taken from your leg. It's a simple plumbing job. The success rate is better than ninety percent."

And there it was: post time in the life-or-death stakes, with my friendly neighborhood bookie calling the odds! I had come to terms with growing old, but this was something different—a face-to-face encounter and a very private dialogue between myself and Brother Death. I had met him twice before, once in Los Angeles in the early sixties and once in Florida in 1980. So, he was not altogether a stranger, nor, curiously enough, was he as frightening as you might imagine. He certainly wasn't welcome, but he wasn't an enemy either. The worst I could say about him was that he was a very untimely visitor.

Now, of course, my wife and my family had to be told. I had affairs to settle, and not too much time to do it. I was a man at risk, and the most time the doctor would grant me was three days at home, "taking things very quietly"—whatever that was supposed to mean. Clearly, I wasn't going any place, and besides I had study to do—a cheery little book of comic cartoons, done in Walt Disney style, showing what was going to happen to me in surgery. Wonderful bedtime reading!

My wife and my family were wonderful—supportive and loving, suppressing their own fears in order not to add to mine. Best of all, they understood what had become for me a new and quite strange imperative. There was fear, of course. There was shame as the body refused its normal functions. There was guilt over life's unfinished business, its unbalanced accounts. There was concern for family and loved ones. There was a need to communicate all this—and all too often, no vocabulary or experience with which to do it. The old Latin tag comments it exactly: *Timor mortis conturbat me*—The fear of death troubles me exceedingly.

At a certain moment I felt a deep need to know that I had discharged all my debts, even to my nearest and dearest, so that I could confront Brother Death in private and learn to be comfortable in his presence. We needed to talk together, get to know each other—because there was always the ten percent chance that our journey together might be to that bourne from which no traveler returns!

Came the day when I was admitted to the Seventh-Day Adventist hospital west of Sydney. It has a splendid cardiac clinic, a well-trained nursing team, and a quite wonderful postoperative support system. They began putting it in place as soon as I arrived. My wife and my sons and daughter were taken in hand by a counselor. They were told what to expect after the operation. They were even taken down to the intensive care ward to prepare them for the sight of me hooked up to tubes and wires, literally as well as figuratively out cold. I had my own counselor, who encouraged me to ask questions. She agreed without hesitation to my formal stipulation that if I collapsed or suffered brain damage, the surgeons would terminate the procedure and let me die. Neither they nor I felt obliged to the officious prolongation of a vegetable life.

Then, carefully and patiently, she began to explain the routines of the operation, the long and merciful anesthesia, the intensive care period, the strange emotional experiences of the aftermath. She explained that, after intensive care, I would be placed in a two-bed ward, with a patient a few days more advanced than I. This was the buddy system, the stronger instructing and supporting the weaker. In due course, I would be expected to take the supporting role. Finally, the counselor and I were talked out. She left. The nurses came in to prepare and premedicate me for the morning's surgery.

My last visitor of the day was the Roman Catholic chaplain whom my wife had called to give me the last rites that the Church administers to those in peril of death. After he had gone, I had the strangest feeling. The act was a piety—good and appropriate. If I died it would be in the house in which I was born. But somehow the act was also redundant. The symbol had already become a reality. The relationship between myself and the Creator was already settled. My personal imperfections had nothing to do with the matter. Alive or dead, I was resting in the hand of Omnipotence. I knew with absolute conviction that I could not fall out of it.

I could not pray. I could only contemplate. The end of that meditation, contemplation, mind-journey, call it what you will, came somewhere in the small hours of the morning. It framed itself something like this: "You gave me life. I didn't ask for it. But, bitter and sweet, you gave it. The gift looks a little bedraggled and defaced now. But while I had it, I loved it. Now, if you want it back, I surrender it, with thanks—and with love for the unknown giver. If at the end you find me unworthy, then, I accept that too. I can do not otherwise."

After that, in some strange way, the sacrament was complete. A final act had been done. I have never felt the need to retract or revise it.

In this fashion, surprising even to myself, I did truly come to terms with dying. I had joined hands with Brother Death, consenting to walk whichever way he led me. My consent was an act of gratitude for all I had been given in life. If now I was to be asked to relinquish it—Amen, so be it, thank you for the gift!

Of the operation itself, I knew nothing. I was anesthetized for the best part of forty-eight hours. I floated back to consciousness by fits and starts, through brief intervals of pain, discomfort, and confusion and vague recollections of movement and voices. I woke to find my wife and children smiling down at me.

The wonder of that moment of waking has never left me. Death had loosed his hold. I was back, surrounded by my loved and loving ones. I was like Lazarus walking out of the tomb to stand blinking and uncertain in the sunlight.

The rush of emotion was too much to bear. I found myself laughing and crying at once, and hurting like hell because my sternum had been sawn asunder, clamped open to let the surgeons do their work, and then sewn together with wire. And that was the second extraordinary sensation—invasion, violation, total and absolute, of my life source. My friend and colleague Jon Cleary, who had undergone a similar intervention, expressed it as "the body weeping for what has been done to it." To which, because he is also a comedian, he added a pungent little afterthought: "Watch out for old ladies in the street, Morris! Their eyesight isn't good. They're liable to bump you!"

This sense of psychic and physical frailty lasted for a long time. I was subject to sudden black depressions and moments of high exaltation. At one moment, I was as dependent as a child seeking reassurance after a nightmare; the next, I was angry and frustrated by my own impotence. My short-term memory became defective; my tolerance of emotional stress was greatly reduced. The controls restored themselves slowly, but my family and I learned to be careful and gentle with one another. My own solution was simply to announce, "Sorry, I'm having a bad day," and then retire to read, rest, or listen to music until the black mist receded.

That was the rough side of the experience. The smooth and shining side was the daily sense of newness, of preciousness. Ask anyone who has survived a cardiac intervention, and you will get the same answer. Every hour of every day is a bonus. You *prize* people. You understand that they are, or can be, as fragile and fearful as you have been—and once they go on the long walk with Brother Death they are lost to you forever. You don't quarrel anymore. You discuss. You don't grasp at things, because, after all, the Creator didn't close His hand on you but let you sit quietly, like a butterfly, on His palm.

As you get stronger, you realize that although you haven't stopped getting older, at least you're aging better and more slowly than you did before. The stairs and hills are easier to climb. You're more attentive in discussion. You listen with more perception. And this time you're not kidding yourself. You are Lazarus Redivivus—Lazarus restored.

There's something else you've learned, too—something a little harder to share. The Lazarus experience is, in effect, a double shuffle. You don't know where and you don't know when, but you know for certain that you've got another meeting with Brother Death and you'll walk away from that one in the opposite direction. The strange thing is that you're not scared anymore. The face of the dark brother is more familiar and more friendly.

This is the essence of what I have tried to express in the novel *Lazarus*, in which I permitted myself to say things I could never have expressed in a personal narrative. Here are the words I put into the mouth of the pontiff:

> There comes a moment when you are aware that you are about to step out of light into darkness, out of the knowing into unknowing, without guarantee of return. It is a moment of clearness and stillness, in which you know, with strange certainty, that whatever is waiting to receive you is good, beneficent, loving. You are aware that you have been prepared for this moment, not by any action of your own, but by the gift of life itself, by the nature of life itself.
>
> When, like Lazarus, I was recalled from the darkness, when I stood blinded by the light of a new day, I knew that my life could never be the same again.
>
> Understand me, dear brothers, I am not talking miracles or private revelations or mystical experiences. I am talking about *metanoia,* that change in the self which takes place, not in contradiction to, but precisely because of, its genetic imprint, the *graffito of God.* We are born to die; therefore, in some mysterious way, we are being prepared for dying. In the same fashion,

we grow towards an accommodation with the greatest mysteries of our existence. Whatever I am, I know that I am not an
envelope of flesh with a soul inside it. I am not Pascal's thinking reed with a ghostly wind whistling through me.

After the change I have described, I was still myself, whole
and entire, but a self renewed and changed by irrigation, as a
seed is changed into a green plant in the dark earth.

Time is not an enemy now. Every moment of it is a priceless
gift.

One of the sweetest moments of my life happened a few
months ago. I was giving a conference to a class of adult university students. When the meeting broke up, a girl in her early
twenties came up to me and said quite simply, "I enjoyed the
talk very much, but most of all I enjoyed seeing a really happy
man."

I hadn't thought of it that way before, but yes, it's true, I'm a
happy man. My life is rich in love, and I still have time to spend
it. How much time, God knows, and I am not pressing him to
tell me. I am a happy spendthrift of the golden days that have
been granted to me.

Which is not to say there are no shadows in my life, no ves-
tiges of anger, no Lazarus memories of the dark days of my
cloistered youth before the stone was rolled away from the
mouth of the tomb and I stood, afraid, blinking at the raw light
of a new world. That sense of strangeness and separateness has
never quite left me.

I confess that sometimes I feel like one of those early travel-
ers who came perhaps from Ephesus to Corinth and made contact with the community of Christian believers in that city. It
was a very different city from the one he had left. Its customs
and attitudes were different. The local community of believers
was not necessarily well disposed to his alien manners. Perhaps

they saw him as a scandalous exotic. Scandal in the assembly is no new thing. Jesus Christ was a stone of scandal. He consorted with tax farmers and public women. The church in Jerusalem very nearly split Christianity by insisting upon circumcision and the kosher killing of meat. The testimony of Paul is, "I withstood Peter to his face."

After the destruction of Jerusalem by the Romans, gentile and Jewish Christian communities abroad were very careful not to identify themselves with Judaean groups, and because of this the early Jewish Christian communities withered away. Despite all these divisions and differences, there existed among believers a fundamental sense of unity. Everybody was a receiver of the good news. Everyone had accepted the Lord Jesus Christ as the one Lord, the Savior. Everyone understood what Paul had meant when he said, "No one can even say Jesus is the Lord unless moved by the Spirit." This receiving of the Spirit, this acknowledgment of the Spirit, was the single unifying factor in all the diversity of peoples, of tongues, of customs and social moralities.

So, as ancient custom dictates, I offer now my own personal testimony. Where do I stand? I am a believer. I was born and baptized into the community of the Roman Catholic Church. All my education conditioned me to belief in the doctrines of the Church—and in many other things that are no part of its essential doctrine. My adult experience forced me to question everything I had been taught. I am still a questioner, because I regard the Christian life as a search and not an arrival. I have not rejected anything that is essential to the profession of faith. I remain, therefore, a Christian and a member of that visible body of Christians which is the Roman Catholic Church.

It is not difficult for me to believe in the existence of God. For me the word *God* is three letters in the Roman alphabet that signify an Unknown and Unknowable who is the active origin of the universe. I do not see, feel, or hear this Unknown in whom, nonetheless, I am aware that I love, move, and have my being. My act of faith is a daily leap through a paper hoop. I think the leap is no less reasonable—and for me it is more reasonable—than the act of those who stand and do not leap. I do not censure them, however. There was a time when to claim that man would fly to the moon was to risk being burned as a magician. Some kind of gift—in the Christian vocabulary it is called a grace—is always needed to make a projection from the known into the unknown.

I believe in the Oneness of God, because in spite of variety and contradiction, I am aware of a unity in the visible universe. A pattern is visible—an evolutionary pattern of growth and development in the physical order and in the order of consciousness. In this pattern the expression *Fatherhood of God* expresses a unity in our origin, a unity in our mutual existence, and a tendency, at least, toward a unified end. I have no quarrel with those women who demand expressions of the deity that encompass their own female selves. I am aware of the lack in every language—and the weight and power of patriarchal imagery. Whatever tends to confirm our sense of unity and harmony, I see as good; whatever tends to destroy it, I see as evil.

I experience humankind as a family, in spite of its murderous disunities. Without love, the human animal becomes subhuman. There is a stamp of love upon the world, however much of it is defaced by hatred and violence. There is a stamp of order upon the whole universe. There is a pulse of eternal energy. There is the mark of a maker. How the making is done, I do not know. But the words of Teilhard de Chardin make a profound sense to me: "God makes things make themselves."

I recite the traditional creed of Nicaea. I cannot, however, explain the incarnation, the death and the resurrection of Christ, the moment of Pentecost, when the first community was fired with the Spirit. It is hard for modern man to enter even into the physical context of the times in which Christ lived and in which his preaching was made. I do not know what happened on the first Easter day. I accept the resurrection on faith through the mouths of apostolic witnesses.

Strangely enough, I am more able to accept these things in the context of an even greater mystery: the mystery of the primal creative act, the why of it, the how of it. If the Godhead has clothed itself with its own creation, the mystery of incarnation would seem a natural part of that primal mystery. It is only when we try to pick it apart with our limited reason and our limited logic that we find ourselves in trouble. In matters of faith, in matters of human destiny, I am content with one all-embracing affirmation: no one falls out of the hand of the living God.

The Church in common speech signifies the visible family of believers. In a larger view it describes the extended family of humankind, clothed in the flesh with which God did not disdain to clothe himself. I am part of that extended family as well.

In a family, hierarchy and authority are natural and necessary. I accept the principle of authority. I insist also on my natural right to challenge the person exercising it if I believe that he or she is misusing it. In the family, mutual respect and service and love are the prime essentials. We are all dependent creatures who cannot make even a decent exit from life without the help of our fellows. "We are all members one of another."

Most, if not all, of the difficulties of the twentieth century arise from the fact that our Church has developed, historically, into something more and something less than a family. It has become an organization, an institution, a highly centralized system. In this, its human aspect, it is very imperfect. Its imperfections lay heavy burdens on the shoulders of the faithful and discourage many folk of goodwill from entering into a communication with it—a communication that for some might develop into a full communion.

The Second Ecumenical Council of the Vatican set in motion a worldwide movement for renewal and reform within the Church, but there is a conviction among many Catholics that the work of renewal is proceeding too slowly and that it is being inhibited by men in authority who are too hidebound by history and have too little care for the service of individual souls—which, after all, is the prime mission of the Church. They plan for tomorrow. We have to accomplish our salvation now. We need the ministry now. Tomorrow we may not be here.

Modern man is mistrustful of authority because he has seen it so hideously abused by totalitarian states. Modern Catholics have developed a correlative mistrust about the usances of power within the hierarchy. They are not rebellious, but they are suspicious. And even though they may express it differently, they understand instinctively the maxim of Saint Bernard of Clairvaux: *Fides suadenda, non imponenda*—Faith must be persuaded and not imposed.

Let me share with you a memory of nearly thirty years ago that is still vivid for me.

The year 1967 was a black time for all of us. The Chinese had exploded their hydrogen bomb. America was committed to its hopeless war in Vietnam. The colonels had seized power in Greece. The shadows of the mushroom cloud seemed to grow darker every day. The hopes of reunion, reconciliation, and *aggiornamento* within the Christian assembly were fading into a twilight of yesterday's compromises by a good Pope who couldn't make up his mind.

We were living then, far from our homeland, in a villa outside the walls of Rome in what was called the Zona Archaeologica. The meadows were littered with antique ruins, and the mountain shepherds from the Abruzzi came there to pasture their flocks in the bitter cold of winter.

It was at first sight a peaceful place, but it was numinous with old and bloody histories. The cypresses grew out of the graves of long-dead men and women. The ashes of forgotten lovers, pillaged from the funerary monuments along the Old Appian Way, nourished the grass verges where modern Romans came to make love in the soft darkness.

In the walled garden of our villa, I would hear the nightingale, which I never saw. I would say the goodnight prayer with our children: "Our Father who art in Heaven . . ." Even as I said it, I would ask myself, "Do you believe what you say? How much do you believe and why? On what terms do you accept the dubious gift of life and the sentence of death that comes with it?"

In the darkness of that near despair, I tried to force myself to remember all that I had been taught as a child and as a man, endowed in a religious family with the gifts of belief and hope and love. In the same moment, I found myself asking whether the gifts were not an illusion: Dead Sea fruit that turned to dust and ashes in the mouth.

"There is a God," my mentors told me, "and the law of God clear down to the smallest tittle of moral and ritual prescription. There is the one hand and the other hand and the Church and the Scriptures to show you how you may walk justly in between."

But if, at the moment when you need Him most, when the bombs begin to fall and the death ovens begin to smoke again and the ministers of God equivocate and God is nowhere to be found, what becomes then of the prophets with their empty promise and the law so abruptly abrogated and justice so easily made a mockery?

I felt suddenly overwhelmed by a storm of anger, of terror, of black despair at the repetitive futility of human effort. It was a dark and dangerous moment, but out of it came my first understanding of the perennial paradox.

Doomed man still struggles to preserve the illusion of immortality, cherishing it as Israel once cherished the ark of the covenant. Man, vilified by abject poverty, deformed by monstrous suffering, still manages to maintain a dignity like a violated temple in a vast and barren desert. Man, debased by tyranny, still dreams of justice—dispenses it, too, in faltering and uncertain fashion. Man, sentenced to death, still plants apple trees whose fruits he will never eat, raises giant cities for other men to live in, stretches upward to a cold moon and secret planets in hostile space. Even the hedonist makes his own defiance of the sorry bargain of life—sweet wine poured out to absent gods, soft kisses spent on golden girls before they wither into toothless crones. Stoicism is another kind of defiance, but in a sense this is the bleakest gesture of all.

The believers are the lucky ones. Like the bull-leapers of ancient Crete, they make a mockery of the death sentence, convinced that one day one last somersault will project them out of the envelope of flesh into a pacific eternity of union with the One who is concealed under the mask of the Many.

In order to survive against the threat of madness in a mad world, to resist the impulse to psychotic fugue from situations too complex to cope with, one has to find a standpoint from which one cannot retreat, from which one may hope to progress to a deeper understanding and a more contented acceptance of one's own existence and the universe that one so briefly inhabits.

It may be the standpoint of the existentialist, who says, "This is what I am. This is all I know. I must, therefore, come to terms with existence for better or for worse." It may be the position of the believer, who says, "I believe thus, and belief gives me all the answers I need to survive." It may be that of the agnostic, who says, "I do not know. I accept not to know."

To arrive at the standpoint involves an act of acceptance, an act of faith or nonfaith—it makes no matter. Without this act, sanity is impossible. There is only the howling confusion of a wasteland.

I know that wasteland. I have heard the black winds that wail across it. I have seen its bleak and barren crags reflected in the eyes of men and women and hurt children. I have learned never to judge any of them, never to close my heart to them or withhold the hand of friendship. I have learned to be grateful for the small candle that lights my own faltering steps and to hope that when it gutters out, I may wake to a final illumination.

> For I am sure that neither death, nor life, nor angels, nor principalities, nor powers, nor things present, nor things to come, nor might, nor height, nor depth, nor any other creature, shall be able to separate us from the love of God which is in Christ Jesus our Lord.

ACKNOWLEDGMENTS

The author wishes to thank Time Inc. for their permission to reprint in full the obituary of His Holiness Pope John XXIII, which *Life* Magazine commissioned and published. His thanks are due also to the Compania Financiera Perlina S.A. and Melaleuka East Investment Pty. Ltd., who own and administer all his copyrights and have permitted the use of certain quotations from speeches and writings incorporated within the body of the text.